FABULOUS FOLDS FOR CARD MAKING™

EDITED BY TANYA FOX

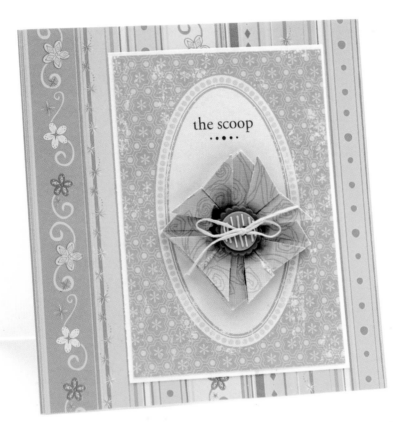

HOUSE of
WHITE
BIRCHES

PUBLISHERS
SINCE 1947

Fabulous Folds for Card Making

EDITOR	Tanya Fox
MANAGING EDITOR	Barb Sprunger
ART DIRECTOR	Brad Snow
PUBLISHING SERVICES DIRECTOR	Brenda Gallmeyer
ASSISTANT ART DIRECTOR	Nick Pierce
COPY SUPERVISOR	Michelle Beck
COPY EDITORS	Amanda Ladig, Susanna Tobias
TECHNICAL EDITOR	Läna Shurb
PHOTOGRAPHY SUPERVISOR	Tammy Christian
PHOTOGRAPHY	Matt Owen, Justin P. Wiard, Kelly Wiard
PHOTOGRAPHY STYLIST	Tammy Steiner
GRAPHIC ARTS SUPERVISOR	Ronda Bechinski
GRAPHIC ARTISTS	Pam Gregory, Erin Augsburger
PRODUCTION ASSISTANTS	Marj Morgan, Judy Neuenschwander
TECHNICAL ARTIST	Nicole Gage

Printed in the United States of America
First Printing: 2009
Library of Congress Number: 2008927496
Hard Cover ISBN: 978-1-59217-231-3
Soft Cover ISBN: 978-1-59217-232-0

DRGbooks.com

Every effort has been made to ensure the accuracy and completeness of the instructions in this book. However, we cannot be responsible for human error or for the results when using materials other than those specified in the instructions, or for variations in individual work.

1 2 3 4 5 6 7 8 9

CONTENTS

For all of you card makers who enjoy learning new techniques, I am pleased to bring you *Fabulous Folds for Card Making*. From some of the most basic folding techniques, such as gatefolds and accordion folds, to more advanced iris folds and designs created with cut-

and-fold templates, there are projects to please every card-making enthusiast and to challenge you enough to take your skill to a new level.

I've always found that folds are a great way to give a basic card design movement and interest. A gatefold card is an ideal design if you're planning to include a gift card. Crafting with cut-and-fold templates is a sure way to turn a simple card into an elegant design. Iris folds are a great way to add a special focal point to your card. And who wouldn't be thrilled to open their card and find a fun, surprise pop-up element?

We've divided this book into six chapters, each one based on an interesting technique, such as gatefolds, iris folds, tea bag folds and pop-up elements. For each chapter, Judi Kauffman has written a brief introduction to the technique, and each project has a clear photo and easy-to-follow instructions. With just a few basic tools and a bit of practice, you'll soon be making these beautiful cards to give to your family and friends.

Happy card making,

Tanya

CONTENTS

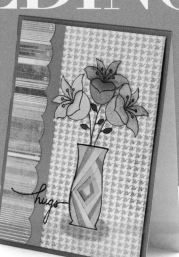

FABULOUS FOLDS FOR CARD MAKING

ACCORDION FOLDS

PAGE 80 Mountains and valleys are the common terms used for the folds on these fast and fun cards.

TEA BAG FOLDS

PAGE 108 Originating from an origami technique, tea bag folding is a must-try for young and old alike.

POP-UPS

PAGE 138 From a single-level pop-up to a multilevel variation, this technique is a great way to create movement in your card design.

CUT AND FOLD

Easy-to-use templates and punches make for quick work when creating fun folded greeting cards like these. You only need a pattern and cutting tool or a punch and a bit of practice to craft these elegant projects.

Safety first: Always keep cutting tools away from children and pets, and take all necessary precautions to safeguard your eyes and hands.

With simple tools and a little time and patience, it's easy to add dimensional pattern elements to a card. You'll need paper or card stock, low-tack removable/reusable tape, a pencil, a cutting mat and a craft knife. You will also need a ruler, a cut-and-fold template or a specially designed punch. If you decide to design your own patterns, you'll need lightweight graph paper as well.

FOLD-em template from POP-UPs by Plane Class

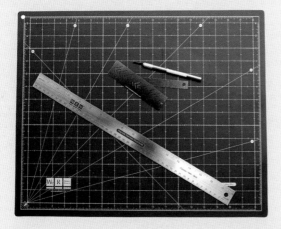

Shown here are the basic tools needed to create cut-and-fold cards: Cutting mat and ruler from We R Memory Keepers, cut-and-fold template; folding aid and craft knife from Plane Class.

Cut-and-fold patterns have been popular with art and math teachers for a long time. Now, thanks to the creativity of designers and manufacturers in the United States and abroad, readily available templates and punches take care of the hard part, which consists of figuring out how the shapes work, where to fold them and how to space and measure between them. If this is your first attempt at making a cut-and-fold card, it's easiest to begin with one of these tools.

Before you get started, here are some helpful tips to keep in mind:

• Practice on inexpensive paper while you are learning the technique.

• Because each kind of paper or card stock cuts and punches differently, it's also a good idea to buy some extra so you can practice on the "real thing" when you are making cards.

• Papers and card stocks with a different pattern or color on each side will produce impressive results. Experiment and have fun learning which papers work best for your project.

Templates

There are three kinds of cut-and-fold templates: plastic, metal and paper.

Durable plastic and metal templates have slits and dotted lines; each slit equals a cutting line, and each dotted line shows where to fold.

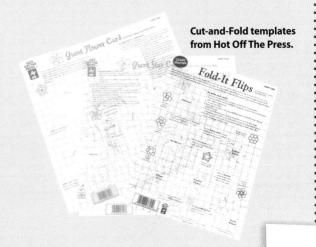

Cut-and-Fold templates from Hot Off The Press.

When using metal templates, the cuts are made while the template is taped in position; with plastic, the slits are used for drawing pencil guidelines, and cuts are made after the template is removed.

Paper templates, available via the internet or photocopied with permission from books and magazines, have solid lines for cutting and dotted lines for folds. These templates can be used only once because you cut through them in order to use them. Make extra copies, one for each card.

1 Protect your work table with a cutting mat.

2 Temporarily tape the card stock or paper to the cutting mat. Next, temporarily tape the template to the card stock or paper. It's important that neither the card stock nor the template moves while you are working. Check to make sure that the template is in the right spot on the card; measure carefully.

3 Make the necessary pencil marks or cuts, depending on which kind of template you used. Double-check to be sure you have completed all cuts or marks before you remove the template.

4 Fold as directed.

Tips

• Use a fresh blade as often as needed to make precise cuts.

• The key to cut-and-fold designs is making sure you have accurate, cleanly cut lines and careful folds. Take your time, and enjoy the process as well as the results.

Punches

Choose specially designed punches that partially cut a shape. The punch does the cutting; you need only fold as instructed. For best results, carefully follow the manufacturer's steps for measuring, positioning the punch, punching and folding. Do not try to use punches with heavier than recommended paper or card stock.

Tumble Punches from Ecstasy Crafts

Dies, Machines & Precut Card Stock

Cut-and-fold dies like those from AccuCut and Ellison are a good way to create patterns without having to do any measuring or cutting by hand. Companies like POP-UPs by Plane Class sell ready-to-fold, precut card-stock pieces. Type the words "cut-and-fold patterns" into your favorite computer search engine and you will find free patterns as well as companies where you can shop for templates and tools.

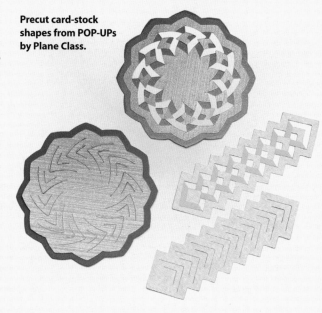

Precut card-stock shapes from POP-UPs by Plane Class.

Design Your Own

If you're feeling adventurous and want to create your own pattern, it helps to work with pencil and lightweight graph paper at the beginning. That way, you can erase, revise, experiment and cut quickly. Part of the fun is seeing how minor adjustments and changes will produce entirely different patterns. You don't have to measure or draw precisely until you like the direction of your design.

Start by drawing six or eight diamonds in a row, end to end, with points touching. Cut the top half of each diamond, fold at the halfway point and bend the diamond back, producing triangular holes next to triangular flaps. You've just created your first cut-and-fold border! Now, start again—but this time, space the diamonds so that they overlap just a bit. When you cut the top half of each diamond this time and fold the cut section back, the shapes look very different. If you alternate the direction of the cutting and folding, tucking the folded shapes between and beneath one another, the results will continue to change. If you cut half-circles instead of diamonds, the look changes yet again. There are endless possibilities, shapes and arrangements. ✸

Resource Guide

FOLD-ems templates and die-cut pre-made FOLD-ems, POP-UPs by Plane Class, www.popuptemplates.com.

Paper Pizazz Diamond, Lattice and other templates, Hot Off The Press, www.paperwishes.com.

Tumble Punches and other punches, Ecstasy Crafts, www.ecstasycrafts.com.

Frantic Stamper (one-stop shopping for templates and punches from a variety of companies), www.franticstamper.com.

Here's an example of an easy make-it-yourself pattern.

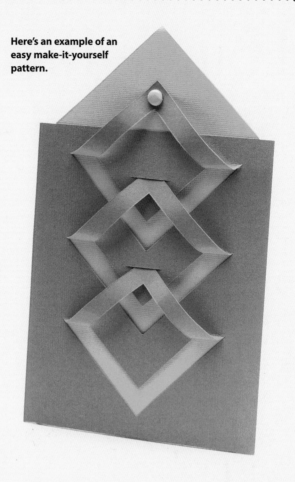

Happy Birthday Star Card

DESIGN BY **SUSAN COBB,** COURTESY OF HOT OFF THE PRESS

1 Trace around giant star template on wrong side of striped paper; cut out.

2 Working clockwise, fold flaps in, tucking flaps under one another; unfold and ink edges blue.

3 In the same manner, trace, cut, fold and ink smaller star using mini star template and teal paper; refold flaps to close star. Punch 1/16-inch hole through center; set aside.

4 *Tag:* Hand-print, or use computer to generate, "Happy Birthday" on yellow dots paper. Position tag template over lettering with lettering toward broad end of tag. Cut out; ink edges blue.

5 *Inside card:* Hand-print, or use computer to generate, "Hope your day is as special as you are" on yellow dots paper. Using blue pen, draw decorative swirl to left of sentiment. Trace around center portion only of giant star, positioning lettering with swirl in center. Cut out; ink edges blue. Adhere inside card.

6 With card unfolded, use giant star template as guide to find center of card; mark lightly and punch 1/16-inch hole. Attach folded paper star and orange silk flower with yellow brad, bending prongs slightly. Place your finger under flower and press to flatten prongs, leaving just enough room to tuck flaps under edges of star to close card.

7 Glue tag to one flap of card as shown. ✳

Sources: Printed papers, flower, brad and template from Hot Off The Press; solvent-based ink from Tsukineko Inc.

Materials

- Citrus Use 'Em for Anything Papers
- Citrus Silk Flowers
- Citrus Brad Pack
- Blue solvent-based ink pad
- Extra-fine-tip pens: black, blue
- Giant Star Card Template (includes templates for mini star and small tag)
- 1/16-inch hole punch
- Computer with printer and font (optional)

Missing You

DESIGN BY **SUSAN COBB,**
COURTESY OF HOT OFF THE PRESS

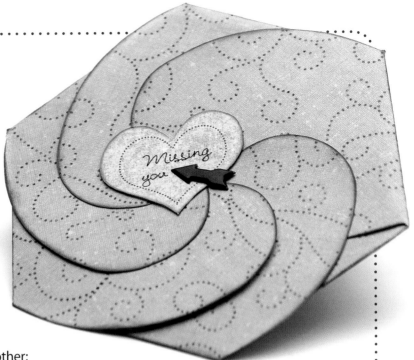

1 Trace around giant spiral template onto wrong side of tan/blue swirls printed paper; cut out.

2 Working clockwise around card, fold flaps in, tucking swirls under one another; unfold again and ink edges.

3 Hand-print, or use computer to generate, "Missing You" on heart die cut, leaving room off to right to attach arrow brad. Punch ¹⁄₁₆-inch hole and attach arrow brad, leaving prongs straight for now.

4 Lay template on reverse side of solid brown paper and trace around hexagonal card center only; cut out. Cut a ½-inch-wide strip from stripes printed paper with stripes running vertically; ink edges and lay strip horizontally across center of brown hexagon. Trim ends even with edges of brown paper; ink edges. Adhere brown center inside card.

FABULOUS FOLDS FOR CARD MAKING

Materials

Finished in a Flash Family
   Scrapbook Page Kit (includes
   printed paper, die cuts and brads)
Brown pigment ink
Extra-fine-tip black permanent marker
Giant Spiral Card Template
Paper piercer or large needle
Paper adhesive
Computer with printer and font
   (optional)

5 *Inside card:* Hand-print, or use computer to generate, "Wish you were here" on bookplate die cut; ink edges. Attach brown mini brads to ends; bend prongs flat. Center and adhere die cut near bottom edge of card center.

6 Using template as a guide, find center of card; mark lightly and punch a ¹⁄₁₆-inch hole. Attach heart die cut with arrow brad, bending prongs slightly. Place your finger under heart and press to flatten prongs, leaving just enough room to tuck flaps under edges of heart to close card. ✹

Sources: Finished in a Flash kit and template from Hot Off The Press; pigment ink from Tsukineko Inc.

Thank You Diamond-Folds Card

DESIGN BY **SUSAN COBB,** COURTESY OF HOT OFF THE PRESS

Project Note

Adhere elements using paper adhesive unless instructed otherwise.

1 Cut a 6½ x 5-inch piece of light blue/brown swirls printed paper with swirls design across top 1¼–2½ inches.

2 Using design that is third from the bottom right on Diamond Folds Template, position design on printed paper ½ inch from right edge and ½ inch from bottom; trace cutting lines with pencil. Move template to left ¾ inch and repeat; repeat to trace a total of six diamonds. Remove template; cut along lines using craft knife.

3 Fold over cut tabs; ink edges brown. Adhere paper to 6½ x 5-inch piece of pink dots printed paper, edges even. Ink outer edges brown.

4 Referring to photo, attach brown mini brads through centers of diamonds as shown. Lightly ink surface of decorative pink brad with dark brown solvent ink to highlight raised design; let dry. Poke brad through silk flower; affix to paper over flower in upper left corner. Affix brown and pink mini brads through centers of pink and brown flowers at top of printed paper. Adhere printed paper to card.

5 Tie knot in center of a 6-inch piece of ribbon; adhere ribbon vertically to card ¼ inch from left edge using adhesive dots. Trim ribbon even with edges of card.

6 Hand-print, or use computer to generate, "Thank You" on pink polka-dot printed paper; trim to 2¼ x ⅞ inches and ink edges brown. For ribbon tab, fold a 1½-inch piece of ribbon in half. Adhere "Thank You" to card ¾ inch from right edge, tucking cut ends of ribbon tab under edge as shown.

7 *Inside card:* Ink edges of tag and 4¼ x 2½-inch piece of pink polka-dot printed paper using brown ink. Hand-print, or use computer to generate, "so very much" on tag. Center and adhere tag to pink rectangle. Attach ⁵⁄₁₆-inch pink brad through end of tag. Attach knotted ribbon at lower right corner of tag using adhesive dots. Center and adhere "so very much" panel inside card. ✸

Sources: Printed papers, Embellish-abilities and template from Hot Off The Press; inks from Tsukineko Inc.

Materials
Bohemian printed papers
6½ x 5-inch white top-fold card
Bohemian Embellish-abilities (includes pink brad, brown and pink mini brads, pink decorative brad, silk flowers, ribbon and tag)
Ink: brown pigment, dark brown solvent
Black extra-fine-tip pen
Diamond Folds Template
Paper piercer or large needle
Craft knife
Small glue dots
Paper adhesive or double-sided tape
Computer with printer and font (optional)

Thinking of You

DESIGN BY **SUSAN COBB,**
COURTESY OF HOT OFF THE PRESS

Materials

Card stock: textured black, white
Chocolate Use 'Em for Anything
   printed papers
5 x 6½-inch white side-fold card
Black ink pad
Chocolate Brad Pack
Chocolate Flowers
Cardmaker's Classic black
   grosgrain ribbon
Black extra-fine-tip pen
Links paper-folding template
Paper piercer or large needle
Craft knife
Small glue dots
Paper adhesive or double-sided tape
Computer with printer and
   font (optional)

Project Note

Adhere elements using paper adhesive unless instructed otherwise.

1 Cover front of card with printed paper. With card closed, trim off upper corners on the diagonal to make tag-shape card. Ink edges.

2 Using template, trace and cut four links from black card stock and three from white card stock. Set aside one black link for card interior. Referring to photo, and alternating colors, attach remaining links, threading one link through the next and folding it in half, to create chain.

3 Attach brown mini brads through white links as shown. Attach larger brown and black silk flowers to chain with brads as shown, attaching black

flower with brown brad and brown flower with black brad. Center and adhere chain to card.

4 Tie brown ribbon in a small bow; trim ends and adhere to card at bottom of chain using adhesive dots.

5 Hand-print, or use a computer to generate, "Thinking of you" on 1½ x 1-inch piece of white card stock; trim corners to create tag. Adhere tag to black card stock and trim, leaving very narrow borders. Adhere tag to card as shown, tucking end under chain.

6 *Inside card:* Hand-print, or use a computer to generate, "On your special day" on white card stock; trim to 3¼ x 1⁵⁄₁₆ inches and ink edges. Center and adhere card stock to a 1³⁄₈ x 3⁵⁄₈-inch piece of printed paper; ink edges. Referring to photo, attach black mini brad through smaller brown flower, reserved black link and end of printed label. Center and adhere label inside card. ✱

Source: Printed papers, flowers, brads, mini brads, flowers, ribbon and template from Hot Off The Press.

Sunburst Card

DESIGN BY **SUSAN COBB,** COURTESY OF HOT OFF THE PRESS

Project Note

Adhere elements using paper adhesive unless instructed otherwise.

1 Adhere yellow printed paper to cover front of card.

2 Cut a 4¾ x 6¼-inch piece from dark pink pin-dot printed paper, positioning dots across bottom 1⅜ inches of piece. Center Diamond Folds 2 template over dark pink area; trace cutting lines with pencil. Remove template; cut along lines using craft knife.

Materials

Use 'Em for Anything Citrus
   printed papers
5 x 6½-inch white card
Citrus Silk Flowers
Citrus Brad Pack
Opaque white ink pen
Diamond Folds 2 template
Paper piercer or large needle
Craft knife
Paper adhesive
Glue dots
Computer with printer and font
   (optional)

3 Fold over cut tabs; adhere tabs to surface of dark pink paper; adhere dark pink paper to card. Poke pink brad through center of yellow daisy; bend prongs flat. Referring to photo, center and adhere daisy to card using a glue dot.

4 *Inside card:* Use Diamond Folds 2 template to trace matching facing designs on ends of 3 x 1½-inch piece cut from dark pink printed paper; cut, fold back and adhere. Adhere dark pink printed paper to yellow printed paper and cut out, leaving ¼-inch borders; adhere to dark pink paper printed and cut out, leaving very narrow borders. Pierce center of each cut, folded design; insert mini brads and bend back prongs. Center and adhere panel inside card.

5 Using opaque white pen, hand-print, or use a computer to generate, "Thank you" on front of card as shown; write "For everything" on panel inside card. ❋

Source: Printed paper, flowers, brads and template from Hot Off The Press.

Best Wishes

DESIGN BY **SUSAN COBB,** COURTESY OF HOT OFF THE PRESS

Project Note

Adhere elements using paper adhesive unless instructed otherwise.

1 Adhere a 5 x 6½-inch piece of gold printed paper to reverse side of an identical piece of brown printed paper with swirls on right edge.

2 Lay paper brown side up; position top center design of Diamond Folds 3 template on brown area 1 inch from left edge and 1⅞ inches from bottom. Trace cutting lines with pencil. Remove template; cut along lines using craft knife.

3 Fold over cut tabs; adhere tabs to surface of brown paper. Using paper piercer, poke hole through paper where smaller folded tabs meet in center; attach brown mini brad through hole.

4 Adhere tan card stock to front of card; adhere cut, folded paper over card stock. Ink edges of a 5 x ¼-inch strip of gold printed paper; adhere to tan card stock and trim, leaving very narrow borders on long edges. Ink edges again and adhere to card ½ inch from bottom.

5 Hand-print, or use computer to generate, "Best wishes" on gold printed paper. Position 2¼ x 1⅛-inch tag template over paper, centering words; trace and cut out. Ink edges. Adhere tag to tan card stock and trim, leaving very narrow edges; ink edges. Referring to photo, center and adhere tag to card as shown.

6 Chalk gold and brown silk leaves; attach brown brad to gold leaf. Adhere leaves to card over upper left corner of tag as shown using small glue dots.

7 *Inside card:* Center and adhere a 5 x 2¾-inch strip of brown printed paper inside card. Hand-print, or use computer to generate, "For a happy birthday" on gold printed paper. Position 3¼ x 1⅝-inch tag template over paper, centering words; trace and cut out. Ink edges. Adhere tag to tan card stock and trim, leaving very narrow edges. Ink edges; attach brown brad to end of tag, then center and adhere tag to paper strip. ❋

Sources: Printed papers, silk leaves, brads and templates from Hot Off The Press; chalks from Craf-T Products; pigment ink from Tsukineko Inc.

Materials
Tan card stock
Autumn Backgrounds printed
　papers
5 x 6½-inch white card
Autumn Silk Leaves
Autumn Brad Pack
Brown pigment ink
Chalks: red, orange
Fine-tip black marker
Diamond Folds 3 Template
Tags Template
Paper piercer or large needle
Craft knife
Paper adhesive
Small glue dots
Computer with printer and font (optional)

Congratulations

DESIGN BY **SUSAN COBB,** COURTESY OF HOT OFF THE PRESS

Project Note

Adhere elements using paper adhesive unless instructed otherwise.

1 Form a 6½ x 5-inch top-folded card from white card stock.

2 Trace Sails design from Fold-it Ribbon Swirls Template onto reverse side of purple textured paper; cut out and punch a ¹⁄₁₆-inch hole in end of each "arm." Bend arms toward center, aligning punched holes and tucking a small piece of foam tape inside bend of each arm for dimension. Attach purple brad through holes and center of flower. Chalk edges.

3 Referring to photo, cut a 6½ x 5-inch piece of lavender/blue/white printed paper, positioning white floral motifs along left side and across bottom. Adhere flower to paper over flower design using foam tape. Punch three ¹⁄₁₆-inch holes through printed swirls and flowers; attach purple mini brads. Adhere paper rectangle to card front.

4 Cut out "Congratulations" sticker; adhere to card front ⅜ inch from right edge and 2½ inches from top. Tie bow from lavender sheer ribbon; adhere to card below "Congratulations" using glue dot. Chalk card edges.

5 *Inside card:* Punch ¹⁄₁₆-inch hole at left end of a 5½ x 1¼-inch strip of lavender/blue/white printed paper; attach purple mini brad and white flower. Center and adhere paper strip to card.

6 Hand-print, or use a computer to generate, "On your Wedding Anniversary" on purple printed paper; trim to 3¾ x ¾ inches, centering words on strip; chalk edges. Adhere strip to white

FABULOUS FOLDS FOR CARD MAKING

Materials

White card stock
Icy Rainbow Creative Pack
    (includes printed paper and
    "Congratulations" sticker)
Icy Rainbow Creative Kit (includes brads,
    mini brads and paper flower)
Black fine-tip marker
Purple chalk
Icy Rainbow Ribbons
Fold-it Ribbon Swirls Template
Craft knife
¹⁄₁₆-inch hole punch
Foam tape
Glue dots
Paper adhesive
Computer with printer and font (optional)

card stock and trim, leaving very narrow borders. Center and adhere words to printed paper strip ¼ inch from right edge.

7 Tie knot in sheer purple ribbon; trim ends and adhere knot to lower left corner of words with glue dot. ✻

Sources: Printed paper, sticker, brads, mini brads, flower, ribbon and template from Hot Off The Press; I Kan'dee chalk from Pebbles Inc.

On your Wedding Anniversary

Gingham Ruffle

DESIGN BY **MARILYNNE OSKAMP,** COURTESY OF ECSTASY CRAFTS INC.

Project Note

Adhere elements using double-sided tape unless instructed otherwise.

1 Photocopy pattern 7 from Tumble Punch book and lay atop blue gingham side of a 4½-inch square cut from card stock.

2 Align Tumble Punch with design on pattern and punch down. Repeat to punch all 13 motifs. Remove pattern.

3 Referring to photo throughout, use your fingers or bone folder to fold back each of the punched designs as shown.

4 Center and adhere punched, folded card stock to card.

Layered Design

1 Press layer 1 of flowers design from 3-D sheet and adhere to card.

2 Press out layer 2; adhere several double-sided adhesive foam squares to reverse side and adhere on top of layer 1.

3 Repeat step 2 to add layers 3 and 4.

Embellishments

1 Adhere line stickers to card near edges of card stock to frame design.

2 Embellish layered design with ultrafine glitter as desired.

3 Tie small bow from ribbon; adhere to card as shown using self-adhesive foam square.

4 Adhere self-stick pearls in corners. ❋

Source: 3-D press-out sheet, sticker sheet, pearls, Tumble Punch, idea/pattern book and foam squares from Ecstasy Crafts Inc.

Materials

Blue solid/blue gingham double-sided card stock
5 x 5-inch side-folded white card-stock card
Pre Cut 3-D sheet – blue hydrangea #P000126
White line sticker sheet #1016
4 self-stick pearls
¼-inch-wide (6mm) off-white sheer ribbon (optional)
Clear iridescent ultrafine glitter (optional)
Tumble Punch round #TU004
Tumble Punch Idea/Pattern Book
Bone folder (optional)
2mm or 3mm double-sided adhesive foam squares
Double-sided tape or paper adhesive

Tumble Punch Flowers

DESIGN BY **MARILYNNE OSKAMP,**
COURTESY OF ECSTASY CRAFTS INC.

Project Note
Adhere elements using double-sided tape unless instructed otherwise.

1 Photocopy pattern 6 from Tumble Punch book and lay atop pink side of a 3½-inch x 5¼-inch rectangle cut from double-sided card stock.

2 Align Tumble Punch with design on pattern and punch down. Repeat to punch all five motifs. Remove pattern.

3 Using your fingers or bone folder, fold back each of the five punched designs.

4 Referring to photo throughout, center and adhere punched, folded card stock to card, positioning punched design along left side.

Layered Design

1 Press layer 1 of iris/ivory flowers design from 3-D sheet and adhere to card.

2 Press out layer 2; adhere several double-sided adhesive foam squares to reverse side and adhere on top of layer 1.

3 Repeat step 2 to add layers 3 and 4.

Embellishments

1 Color line stickers green and purple with markers. Adhere purple line stickers around edges of pink card stock to frame design. Adhere green line stickers around edges of off-white card.

2 Tint "Best Wishes" sticker from Multiple Sayings sticker sheet with purple marker; adhere to pink card stock below punched designs.

Materials
Umbrella pink solid/purple polka
  dots double-sided card stock (#34273)
4 x 5⅞-inch side-folded ivory
  card-stock card
Pre Cut 3-D Sheet – tropical flowers
  #P000138
Gold metallic sticker sheets: line #1082,
  Multiple Sayings #345
5 self-stick purple pearls
Clear iridescent ultrafine glitter (optional)
Permanent markers: green, purple
Tumble Punch flower #TU002
Tumble Punch Idea/Pattern book
Bone folder (optional)
2mm or 3mm double-sided adhesive
  foam squares
Double-sided tape or paper adhesive

3 Embellish layered design with ultrafine glitter as desired.

4 Adhere self-stick pearls in center of punched motifs as shown. ✺

Sources: Card stock from American Crafts; 3-D press-out sheet, sticker sheets, pearls, Tumble Punch, idea/pattern book and foam squares from Ecstasy Crafts Inc.

Blossom Punch Mailbox Card

DESIGN BY **MARILYNNE OSKAMP,** COURTESY OF ECSTASY CRAFTS INC.

Project Note

Adhere elements using double-sided tape unless instructed otherwise.

1 Form a 5¾ x 4⅛-inch top-folded card from ivory textured card stock.

2 Cut a 1¾ x 4⅛-inch strip of light yellow card stock; adhere to card ⅜ inch from right edge.

Punched Blossoms

1 Photocopy pattern 2 from pattern book; center punch-shaped parts of pattern on a 1⅜ x 3⅞-inch strip of textured coral card stock. Align blossom punch with its punch design on pattern and punch down. Repeat to punch shapes at top and bottom of strip.

2 Remove pattern. Using your fingers or bone folder, fold back petals.

3 Using the same pattern and procedure, punch three blossoms from light pink card stock, leaving at least 1 inch between punched designs. Cut out punched designs, leaving a ½-inch border around petals. Adhere punched designs behind openings in coral card stock, alternating pink and coral petals; fold back pink petals.

4 Center punch-shaped parts of pattern 2 on a 1¼ x 3¾-inch strip of dark yellow card stock. Align blossom punch with its punch design on pattern and punch down. Repeat to punch shapes at top and bottom of strip. Do not fold petals back; adhere dark yellow card stock behind coral card stock so that yellow petals are centered in punched blossoms.

5 Center and adhere punched strip to light yellow strip on card.

Materials

Card stock: ivory textured, light yellow, yellow, coral textured, light pink
6 x 4-inch top-folded ivory card-stock card
Girl-with-mailbox images from 3-D Diecut Morehead Clown/letter/kitty with cake #11052321
Gold metallic line sticker sheet #1016
3 (³⁄₃₂-inch) orange square self-adhesive jewels
Clear iridescent ultrafine glitter (optional)
Blossom Punch Idea/Pattern book
Blossom punch #BP001
Craft knife
Bone folder (optional)
Photocopier
2mm or 3mm double-sided adhesive foam squares
Double-sided tape

Layered Design

1 Referring to photo throughout, adhere layer 1 of 3-D girl-with-mailbox design to card.

2 Adhere several double-sided adhesive foam squares to reverse side of layer 2; adhere on top of layer 1.

3 Repeat step 2 to add layers 3–13.

Embellishments

1 Adhere self-stick jewel on the diagonal in center of each punched blossom.

2 Embellish layered design with ultrafine glitter as desired.

3 Adhere line stickers to card as desired. ✹

Source: 3-D die-cut girl with mailbox images, line sticker sheet, jewels, Blossom Punch Idea/Pattern book, Blossom Punch and foam squares from Ecstasy Crafts Inc.

Pink Rose Card

DESIGN BY **MARILYNNE OSKAMP,** COURTESY OF ECSTASY CRAFTS INC.

Project Note

Adhere elements using double-sided tape unless instructed otherwise.

1 Cut a 1⁷⁄₁₆ x 5-inch strip of moss green card stock; adhere strip vertically to card ³⁄₁₆ inch from right edge.

2 Center stencil on reverse side of a 1³⁄₁₆ x 4¾-inch strip of shimmering pink card stock; secure with removable tape. Lay stencil and card stock on piercing pad. Pierce design—the dots between the cutting slots—using the piercing tool.

3 Using craft knife, cut folding design by sliding knife blade into each slot and cutting out from each corner. Check reverse side of card stock to make certain all lines have been cut. Remove stencil and tape.

4 Referring to photo throughout, use your fingers or bone folder to fold each of the five cut designs.

5 Embroider pierced designs using 1 strand metallic thread and securing thread ends on the reverse side with tiny pieces of single-sided tape.

Note: *On front of stitched design, holes have smooth edges; on reverse side, edges of holes are slightly raised.*

6 Center and adhere cut, folded, embroidered design to moss green card-stock strip on card.

Layered Design

1 Adhere layer 1 of three-dimensional rose design to card.

2 Adhere several double-sided adhesive foam squares to reverse side of layer 2; adhere on top of layer 1. **Option:** *Before attaching foam squares, gently curl edges of layer 2 over the dull blade of a pair of scissors to give them realistic dimension.*

3 Repeat step 2 to add remaining layers.

4 Adhere a few adhesive foam squares to reverse side of butterfly and adhere to card as shown.

Embellishments

Adhere gold line stickers to moss green card stock next to edges of shimmering pink card stock. Adhere another line sticker near card fold. ✳

Source: 3-D diecut roses and butterfly, line sticker sheet, stencil and foam squares from Ecstasy Crafts Inc.

Materials
Card stock: moss green,
   shimmering light pink
5 x 5-inch side-folded pale pink card-
   stock card
3-D Diecut Roses #82101
Gold metallic line sticker sheet #1016
Dark red/pink metallic thread
Cisioo stencil (CI005)
Very fine piercing tool
Piercing pad
Needle with small eye
Craft knife
Bone folder (optional)
2mm or 3mm double-sided adhesive
   foam squares
Tape: double-sided, removable

Christmas Polka-Dots Card

DESIGN BY **MARILYNNE OSKAMP,**
COURTESY OF ECSTASY CRAFTS INC.

Materials

Red card stock
Black-and-white polka-dot double-sided
    printed paper
5 x 5-inch side-folded white
    card-stock card
3-D Diecut Morehead Puppies in Boot
    #11052324
Sticker sheets: white and black lines
    #1016, ⅛-inch gold holographic circles
Self-stick round green jewels
Clear iridescent ultrafine glitter (optional)
Fine-tip green permanent marker
Incire stencil #IC0045
Cutting mat or piece of glass
Craft knife
Bone folder (optional)
2mm or 3mm double-sided adhesive
    foam squares
Tape: double-sided, removable

Project Note
Adhere elements using double-sided tape unless instructed otherwise.

1 Center and adhere a 4¾-inch square of red card stock to card.

2 Center stencil on right side of a 4⅝-inch-square piece of polka-dot paper and secure on reverse side with removable tape. Lay stencil and paper on cutting mat. Using craft knife, cut out folding design by sliding knife blade into each slot and cutting out from each corner. Check reverse side of card stock to make certain all lines have been cut. Remove stencil and tape.

3 Referring to photo throughout, use your fingers or bone folder to fold back each of the cut designs as shown.

4 Center and adhere cut, folded design to card.

Layered Design

1 Adhere layer 1 of puppy design to card.

2 Adhere several double-sided adhesive foam squares to reverse side of layer 2; adhere on top of layer 1. *Option: Before attaching foam squares, gently curl edges of layer 2 over the dull blade of a scissors to give them realistic dimension.*

3 Repeat step 2 to add remaining layers.

Embellishments

1 Adhere white line stickers over edges of polka-dot printed paper. Adhere black line stickers around edges of card, centering them in the white border.

2 Embellish layered design with ultrafine glitter as desired.

3 Color 18 gold dot stickers with green marker; adhere stickers to folded-back points. *Option: Substitute adhesive jewels for some or all stickers.*

4 Adhere three jewels for puppy's necklace. ✸

Sources: Printed paper from Making Memories; 3-D die-cut puppies, line sticker sheet, jewels, stencil and foam squares from Ecstasy Crafts Inc.

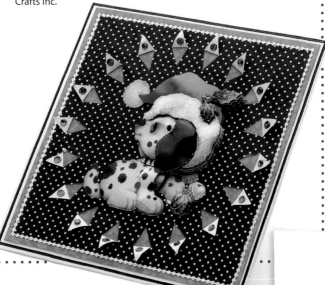

Get Well Lattice-Fold Card

DESIGN BY **KATHLEEN PANEITZ**

5 Referring to photo and alternating patterns, arrange lattice sections on card, beginning with an orange section at bottom and overlapping sections to create lattice design; adhere lattice to card.

6 Poke mini brad through tag and hydrangea blossom; affix to card as shown.

7 Poke mini brads through remaining hydrangea blossoms and affix to card as shown. ✳

Sources: Printed papers from A2Z Essentials; hydrangea blossoms, brads and tag from Making Memories; decorative-edge scissors from Fiskars; 1¼-inch punch from EK Success Ltd.; 1½-inch punch from Uchida of America.

1 Form a 5 x 4¼-inch top-folded card from white card stock.

2 Trim long edges of a 5 x 3¼-inch piece of card stock using decorative-edge scissors; center and adhere to a 5 x 3⅝-inch piece of green-on-green printed paper; center and adhere paper to card.

3 Punch four 1¼-inch squares at least ¾ inch apart on orange/light blue double-sided printed paper. Center 1½-inch punch around each punched square and punch again, creating 4 square frames.

4 Cut frames in half on the diagonal, creating eight V-shape lattice sections.

Materials

Card stock: white, dark orange
What's New Club double-sided printed papers: Floral Zest 2 and 3
3 (1¼-inch) green paper hydrangea blossoms
3 white mini brads
1-inch "get well" white epoxy tag
Square paper punches: 1¼-inch, 1½-inch
Clouds decorative-edge scissors
Craft knife
Paper adhesive

Pink Romance Card

DESIGN BY ROBIN ARNOLD

1 Lay card stock black side up; score horizontally 3⅞ inches from top and fold down to form 8 x 4⅛-inch top-fold card with black showing along bottom edge.

2 Lightly draw a horizontal line on card front ¾ inch below fold. Mark on fold 1¼ inches from left side, then every ¼ inch thereafter, making last mark ¾ inch from right edge.

3 Using scissors or craft knife, cut diagonally through both layers of card stock from each mark on fold to line below, keeping cuts parallel to one another.

4 Erase line and all marks.

5 Open card and lay flat. Beginning at one end, fold every other tab to the left, tucking point of folded-down tab (black) behind next unfolded tab (pink). Close card.

6 Referring to photo, affix rhinestone brad through center of black flourish die cut; center and adhere flourish die cut to card as shown. Adhere corner die cuts to corners of card. Adhere alphabet stickers to card to spell "romance." ✻

Materials
8-inch square of scallop-edge pink/black double-sided card stock
Card-stock die cuts: 4¾ x 2-inch black flourish, 2 (1¼ x 1¼-inch) pink-and-black pin-dot photo corners
½-inch pink-and-black alphabet stickers to spell "romance"
Decorative rhinestone brad
Paper adhesive

Happy Day! Card

DESIGN BY **LISA SILVER**

Materials

Card stock: ivory shimmery, blue-gray
Blue-gray, burgundy and tan floral/burgundy solid double-sided printed paper
Classic Essential Expressions "OH HAPPY DAY!" stamp
Ink: dark gray distress, blue-gray
Fine silver cord
⅜-inch pearl cabochon
Blue-gray eyelet
Bone folder or straight edge
Eyelet-setting tool
Punches: 2-inch circle, 1½ x ⅜-inch word punch
Sewing machine and white thread
Paper adhesive
Mini glue dots

Project Note

Adhere elements using paper adhesive unless instructed otherwise.

1. Cut and fold blue-gray card stock to form a 5-inch-square top-fold card.

2. Punch nine 2-inch circles from double-sided paper. Set aside one circle to use as base for flower.

3. *Flower petal:* Fold one circle into quarters. With printed side facing up and fold lines running horizontally and vertically, fold curves in on lower half of circle to form point at bottom edge (see Fig. 1 on page 173).

4. Flip circle over so solid burgundy side faces up. Fold sides toward each other so that folds created in step 3 meet in center (see Fig. 2 on page 173).

5. Repeat steps 3 and 4 with remaining circles to make a total of eight petals. Burnish folds with bone folder.

6. Arrange petals on reserved circle to form flower, tucking inner petals under adjacent petals as necessary; adhere to base circle.

7. Center and adhere flower to 4-inch square of gray-blue card stock, then to 4¾-inch square of floral printed paper. Using a small zigzag stitch, machine-stitch over edge of blue-gray square.

8. Center and adhere flower to card. Adhere pearl cabochon in center with glue dot.

9. *Tag:* Stamp "OH HAPPY DAY!" on ivory shimmery card stock using distress ink. Punch word window around words, leaving room at left end for eyelet; ink tag edges blue-gray. Set eyelet in tag; thread silver cord through eyelet and tie around pearl. Adhere tag to flower with glue dot. ✱

Sources: Shimmery card stock from CutCardStock.com; blue-gray card stock and word window tag punch from Stampin' Up!; printed paper from My Mind's Eye; stamp from Cornish Heritage Farms; distress ink from Ranger Industries; eyelet from Making Memories.

May You Find Courage

DESIGN BY **SANDRA GRAHAM SMITH**

Project Note

Adhere elements using paper adhesive unless instructed otherwise.

1 Cut and fold sage card stock to form a 4¼ x 5½-inch side-fold card.

2 Photocopy or trace lattice-fold pattern, page 173; using removable tape, secure pattern to

card with dashed line along fold. Cut along diagonal pattern lines using craft knife. Remove pattern.

3 Open card and lay flat. Carefully fold down each large cut tab. Close card.

4 Stamp sympathy sentiment on card with text 1⅝ inches from right edge.

5 Punch three square flourish motifs from dark green card stock. Thread a ¾ x 5½-inch strip of black card stock through motifs as shown, belt-buckle style. Referring to photo, adhere motifs and strip to card along right edge.

6 *Inside card:* Stamp "God bless you …" sentiment onto a 2⅜ x 1-inch rectangle cut from dark green card stock; center and adhere inside card. ✳

Sources: Vertical "Sympathy" stamp from Paper Inspirations; "God bless you …" stamp from Rubbernecker; square flourish punch from McGill Inc.

Burgundy Elegance

DESIGN BY **JERRY STEVENS,** COURTESY OF PLANE CLASS

Project Note

Adhere elements using paper adhesive unless instructed otherwise.

1 Form a 5½ x 4¼-inch top-folded card from burgundy card stock.

2 Using removable tape, adhere template to shimmering pink card stock. Holding the craft knife perpendicular to paper, cut all slits in template pattern. **Note:** *When cutting slits that meet to form a corner, cut from the corner out in both directions to ensure a clean cut and sharp corner.*

3 Remove template and tape. Note pattern of larger and smaller cuts, which will form larger and smaller tabs. Using folding aid, fold the larger tabs over, tucking them under the adjacent smaller tabs.

Materials

Card stock: burgundy solid,
   shimmering pink/flat pale pink
   double-sided
Metallic Stripes red/purple on black
   lightweight textured paper
Peel-Off silver metallic stickers: dots
   #0841s, 1¼-inch corners #3481j
FOLD-em template #1
Folding Aid
Craft knife with #16 blade
Removable tape
Paper adhesive

4 Referring to photo, cut around cut-and-folded design, creating a 5⅛ x 1⅜-inch panel with points at ends and "teeth" along top and bottom edges that mimic the pattern of cuts and folds.

5 Adhere cut, folded paper to Metallic Stripes card stock. Trim around design leaving ³⁄₁₆-inch border. Center and adhere to card on the diagonal.

6 Adhere silver dot stickers to points of cut, folded design; adhere corner stickers in opposite corners of card. ❋

Source: Lightweight textured paper, stickers, template and folding aid from POP-UPs by Plane Class.

Floral Happy Birthday

DESIGN BY **JERRY STEVENS,**
COURTESY OF PLANE CLASS

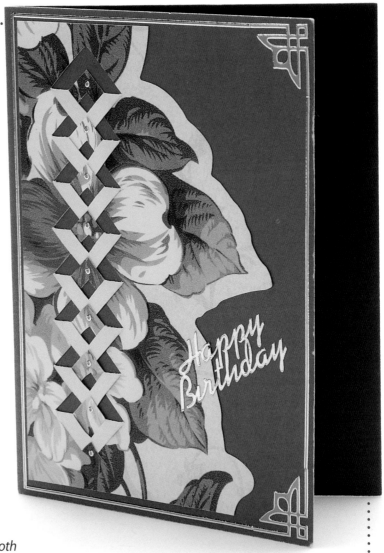

Project Note

Adhere elements using paper adhesive unless instructed otherwise.

1 Form a 4¼ x 5½-inch side-folded burgundy card from card stock.

2 Using removable tape, center and adhere template to a 5⅛ x 3½-inch piece cut from wallpaper border. Holding craft knife perpendicular to paper, cut all slits in template pattern.
Note: *When cutting slits that meet to form a corner, cut from the corner out in both directions to ensure a clean cut and sharp corner.*

3 Remove template and tape. Note the pattern of larger and smaller cuts, which will form larger and smaller tabs. Using folding aid, fold down larger tabs, tucking them under adjacent smaller tabs.

4 Referring to photo, adhere cut, folded wallpaper border to card ³⁄₁₆ inch from fold and top and bottom.

5 Adhere gold dot stickers (reserved from scrap areas of sticker sheet) to points of cut, folded design; adhere "Happy Birthday," line and corner stickers to card as shown. ✹

Source: Stickers, template and folding aid from POP-UPs by Plane Class.

Materials

Burgundy/dark green
   double-sided card stock
Floral wallpaper
Peel-Off gold metallic stickers: dots,
   straight lines #0841g, corners #0842g,
   "Happy Birthday" #0300g
FOLD-em template #2
Folding aid
Craft knife with #16 blade
Removable tape
Paper adhesive

Best Wishes

DESIGN BY **JERRY STEVENS,** COURTESY OF PLANE CLASS

Project Note
Adhere elements using paper adhesive unless instructed otherwise.

1 Form a 4¼ x 5½-inch side-folded card from shiny black card stock.

2 Using removable tape, adhere template to printed side of gold/silver/black Metallic Stripes card stock. Holding craft knife perpendicular to paper, cut all slits in template pattern. **Note:** *When cutting slits that meet to form a corner, cut from the corner out in both directions to ensure a clean cut and sharp corner.*

3 Remove template and tape. Note pattern of larger and smaller cuts, which will form larger and smaller tabs. Using folding aid, fold over larger tabs, tucking them under adjacent smaller tabs.

4 Referring to photo, cut around the cut, folded design, leaving a ³⁄₁₆-inch border.

5 Adhere cut, folded paper to red/violet/black Metallic Stripes card stock. Trim around design leaving ³⁄₁₆-inch border. Adhere to card ³⁄₁₆ inch from top.

6 Adhere silver dot stickers (reserved from scrap areas of sticker sheet) to cut, folded design; adhere daisy to center. Adhere "Best Wishes" and corner stickers as shown. ❋

Source: Metallic Stripes card stock, stickers, template and folding aid from POP-UPs by Plane Class.

Materials
Card stock: shiny black, Metallic Stripes gold/silver/black and red/violet/black
Peel-Off silver metallic stickers: ⅞-inch daisy (flower pot set) #1031s, 1-inch corners #3901j, "Best Wishes" #0309s, silver dots
FOLD-em template #3
Folding aid
Craft knife with #16 blade
Removable tape
Paper adhesive

Dragonfly Card

DESIGN BY **ROBIN ARNOLD**

Project Note

Adhere elements using paper adhesive unless instructed otherwise.

1 Form a 5½ x 4-inch top-folded card from ard stock.

2 Copy or trace folding pattern on page 173. Center and adhere paper-folding template to a 2¼ x 5½-inch piece of textured paper using removable tape. Cut along template pattern lines using a craft knife.

3 Remove template and tape. Fold down top tab and every other tab thereafter, tucking points behind adjacent upright tabs.

Materials
Ivory card stock
Light brown alligator-skin textured paper
Peel-Off gold metallic stickers: 1-inch
    dragonfly #1019g, lines #0841g
Diagonal paper-folding template
Craft knife
Removable tape
Paper adhesive

4 Referring to photo, adhere cut, folded paper to card ¼ inch from fold. Adhere line stickers over edges of textured paper; adhere dragonfly as shown. ✳

Source: Peel-Off stickers from POP-UPs by Plane Class.

GATEFOLD

Simple folds like these are one of the easiest and fastest ways to add dimension or movement to handmade cards. For gatefolds and fold-back cards, only card stock, a folding tool and your imagination are needed for results that are one-of-a-kind.

Like double doors or divided gates, gatefold and fold-back cards invite you to open them and see what's inside.

Gatefold

The most common kind of gatefold cards opens from the left and the right, with folds at the sides, the two flaps meeting in the middle. But there are no rules that the dividing line has to be in the center and that the flaps have to be the same size or can't overlap.

Basic gate fold card.

There are five possible flat surfaces to embellish: the two flaps (front and back of both of the side panels) and the center inside panel that you see as soon as the card is open. Most gateold cards focus attention on the front flaps and center inside panel, leaving the inside of each flap a solid color, but those two extra inside panels offer space for decorative papers, text, stamping, pockets and more.

Remember, although gatefold cards are simple and easy to make, careful, accurate measuring and scoring are very important.

Fold-Back

Fold-back cards are much like gatefold cards in that they are usually symmetrical and they often open in the center, but there's a twist. Each

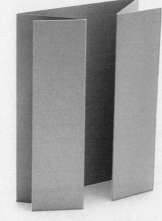

Basic fold-back card.

flap has added dimension, a layer that folds back like a collar on a jacket. In fact, fold-back cards that look like shirts, tuxedo jackets or fancy dresses are some of the most popular.

Other fold-back flaps include shapes like leaves, flowers, holiday trees, or geometric shapes like squares, triangles and half-circles. The possibilities are endless.

To keep a fold-back card closed, consider wrapping it with a paper or card-stock band or adding a ribbon or cord to tie it shut.

The Envelope, Please

For both gatefold and fold-back cards, start with a standard-size envelope and make cards that fit inside, unless you want to make custom envelopes or use envelopes that require additional postage, i.e. square or oversized envelopes. Standard A2, A6 and A7 envelopes are popular and easy to find.

Make sure your card is smaller than the envelope so it is easy to insert and remove. This is especially important if you are using dimensional elements or lots of layers.

Tips & Ideas

To change the look of a card, choose a different color combination and vary the embellishments. A fold-back black tuxedo with black bow tie and white shirt can easily become a professorial plaid jacket with polka-dot bow tie. A man's Hawaiian shirt with a floral print can turn into a woman's blouse with a lacy patterned paper and trim at the collar and sleeves. Turn a fold-back Christmas tree into a Deco-inspired geometric triangle topped with half-circles and mini dots. Turn a flower-encrusted gatefold into a winter scene with snowflakes. ✱

Best of Luck Card

DESIGN BY **LINDSEY BOTKIN**

Project Note
Adhere elements using paper adhesive unless instructed otherwise.

1. Vertically score an 8½ x 4¼-inch piece of white card stock 2⅛ inches from both sides; fold ends toward center to form a 4¼-inch-square gatefolded card.

2. Center and adhere a 1⅞ x 4-inch piece of Home paper floral side up to each front panel.

3. Stamp "best of luck" onto bottom right corner of a 3-inch square of white card stock. Center square on front of card ⅝ inch from top edge; adhere to left panel only.

4. Stamp butterfly onto blue side of Home paper; cut out and adhere to white square, overlapping top and left edges, using dimensional glue dots.

5. Punch a ¹⁄₁₆-inch hole in right panel of card 1¼ inches from top and ⅜ inch from fold; attach photo turn with mini brad; use photo turn to hold card closed.

6. *Inside card:* Center and adhere a 4-inch square of brown floral Home paper to card. Ink flower portion of daisies stamp with blue marker and leaves with dark brown; stamp image onto

Materials
White card stock
Home printed paper
Stamps: butterfly, "Best of Luck," three
   daisies
Black solvent-based ink
Stamp markers: blue, dark brown
Pewter mini brad
Pewter photo turn
Punches: ¹⁄₁₆-inch hole, word window
Dimensional glue dots
Paper adhesive

bottom right corner of a 3¼-inch square of white card stock. Adhere card stock to bottom right corner of printed paper, leaving narrow borders. Stamp a word window from blue side of Home paper; cut off a 1-inch piece and adhere inside card, overlapping upper left corner of white card-stock square. ✱

Sources: Card stock, markers, photo turn and word window punch from Stampin' Up!; printed paper from My Mind's Eye; stamps from Inkadinkado; solvent-based ink from Tsukineko Inc.

Snowman Surprise Card

DESIGN BY **ROBIN ARNOLD**

4 Stamp snowflakes around edges of a 3½-inch square of white card stock using blue ink; cut a 2⅝ x 2⅞-inch piece from center. Discard center or reserve for another use.

5 Adhere ribbon to a 2⅜ x 2⅝-inch piece of blue card stock, centering snowman image on card stock and wrapping excess ribbon to reverse side. Center and adhere ribbon-covered card stock to a 2½ x 2¾-inch piece of black card stock.

6 Close card. Referring to photo, center card stock with snowman ribbon on front of card; adhere to left panel only.

7 Center stamped white and blue card-stock frames on front of card; adhere blue frame to left panel only; adhere white frame to right panel only, making sure frames move freely when card is opened. ❋

Source: Snowflakes rubber stamp from Stampin' Up!

1 Vertically score an 8½ x 4¼-inch strip of red card stock 2⅛ inches from left edge and 2⅛ inches from right edge. Fold ends toward center to form 4¼-inch-square gatefold card.

2 Stamp snowflakes around edges of a 4¼ x 4-inch piece of blue card stock using white ink.

3 Cut a 3½-inch square from center of stamped blue card stock; reserve blue card-stock frame. Stamp snow people sentiment across top of blue square using black ink. Center and adhere square inside card.

Sailboat Cards

DESIGNS BY **MARY AYRES**

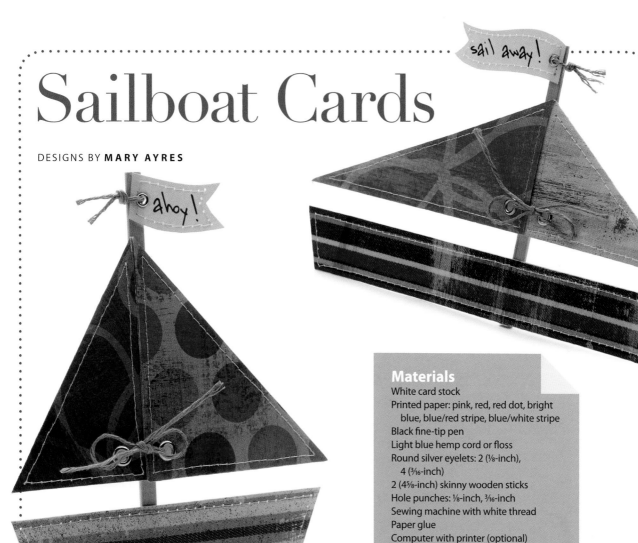

Materials
White card stock
Printed paper: pink, red, red dot, bright blue, blue/red stripe, blue/white stripe
Black fine-tip pen
Light blue hemp cord or floss
Round silver eyelets: 2 (⅛-inch), 4 (³⁄₁₆-inch)
2 (4⅝-inch) skinny wooden sticks
Hole punches: ⅛-inch, ³⁄₁₆-inch
Sewing machine with white thread
Paper glue
Computer with printer (optional)

Long Boat

1 Referring to patterns, pages 172 and 173, trace entire long sail onto wrong side of pink printed paper; cut out. Score sail along dashed lines and fold sides toward center so that pink sails show on front.

2 Cut large sail section only from red printed paper; adhere to matching section of pink sail.

3 Cut long boat from blue/red stripe printed paper.

4 Hand-print, or use a computer to generate, "sail away!" on white card stock. Cut large flag shape around words.

5 Using a straight stitch, machine-stitch around flag, boat and front sections of sail, stitching ⅛ inch from edge.

6 Punch a ⅛-inch hole in flag and ³⁄₁₆-inch holes in sail where indicated by dots on patterns. Attach eyelets in holes.

7 Adhere flag to stick at top and boat at bottom with ends of stick even with top edge of flag and bottom edge of boat. Adhere sail to stick ⅜ inch above boat.

8 Tie cord around mast and through eyelet in flag; knot and trim ends. Tie cord through eyelets in sail to hold sail closed; tie ends in a bow.

Short Boat

Using patterns on pages 172 and 173, follow instructions for Long Boat, cutting entire sail from bright blue printed paper, large section of sail from red dot, and boat from blue/white stripe. Hand-print, or use a computer to generate, "ahoy!" on small flag. ✸

Source: Skinny wooden craft sticks from Forster Craft.

37

Birds Galore Pocket Card

DESIGN BY **LINDSEY BOTKIN**

Materials

White card stock
Double-sided printed paper: tan/white
   with polka dots, coral/light green
   floral, sky blue/multicolor swirls
Birds Galore clear stamp set
Black solvent-based ink
Colored markers
Blender pen
White gel pen
½-inch-wide sheer white polka-dot
   ribbon
2 (½-inch) pewter eyelets
3 pewter mini brads
Paper piercer
Punches: corner rounder, 1⁄16-inch hole,
   ¼-inch hole, word window
Dimensional glue dots
Paper adhesive

Project Note

Adhere elements using paper adhesive unless instructed otherwise.

Pocket

1. Lay a 12 x 5½-inch piece of polka-dot printed paper with dots facing up; score vertically 4 inches from right side and 4 inches from left side.

2. Beginning at top, cut down 1⅜ inches on each fold. From that point, cut outward and down in a straight diagonal line to adjacent bottom corner, forming pointed flaps. Fold flaps to center, overlapping points; adhere points and bottom edge to form pocket. Round off upper corners of pocket with punch.

3. Wrap a 9 x 1¼-inch strip of light green floral paper around pocket ⅜ inch from bottom, overlapping ends on back; adhere. Center and adhere a 4¼ x ⅝-inch strip of polka-dot paper to celery strip.

Sky Blue Tag

1. Round off upper corners of a 4½ x 2¾-inch piece of sky blue paper.

2. Stamp bird with trailing flowers onto polka-dot paper; color using markers. Trim paper to 2¾ x 2½ inches; adhere to tag ⅛ inch from bottom.

3. Adhere 2¾ x ⅝-inch strip of coral paper to polka-dot paper above bird. Using gel pen, draw a straight line across center of coral strip. Use piercing tool to make "needle holes" along line.

4. Punch a ¼-inch hole centered near top edge; set eyelet in hole. Knot ribbon through eyelet.

Coral/Light Green Tag

1. Round off upper corners of a 2⅞ x 4¾-inch piece of coral paper.

2. Stamp flock of birds on light green floral paper; trim paper to 2½ x 4½-inches. Round off upper corners; center and adhere to coral tag.

3. Punch two word windows from coral paper; referring to photo, trim off one end of each and adhere to tag along right side with straight ends even with edge of light green floral paper. Punch ¹⁄₁₆-inch holes through tabs near rounded ends; insert mini brads.

4. Punch a ¼-inch hole centered near top edge of tag; set eyelet in hole. Knot ribbon through eyelet. ✹

Sources: Card stock, eyelets, piercing tool and Pop Up Glue Dots from Stampin' Up!, printed papers from Crate Paper; stamp set from Inkadinkado; solvent-based ink from Tsukineko Inc.; markers and blender pen from Copic; ribbon from Making Memories; corner rounder punch from Creative Memories.

4. Punch a ¹⁄₁₆-inch hole through strips near left edge; insert mini brad.

5. Using gel pen, draw a straight line across bottom of pocket near edge. Use piercing tool to make "needle holes" along line to give the appearance of stitching.

6. Stamp bird with trailing flowers onto white card stock; color using markers and cut out. Adhere over strips using dimensional glue dots.

Spring Door

DESIGN BY **LINDA BEESON**

Project Note

Adhere elements using paper adhesive unless instructed otherwise.

1 Form a 5¾ x 6-inch top-folded card from card stock. Ink edges pink and chestnut.

2 Trim a 5½ x 5¾-inch piece of Suffuse paper using decorative-edge scissors; center and adhere to card.

3 Center tag template vertically on a 5⅜ x 5½-inch piece of Season paper. Using craft knife, cut across bottom of template and around curved top, leaving sides uncut. Remove template; cut down center of tag and fold back sides to create window. Ink all edges pink and chestnut.

4 Center and adhere a 4 x 5½-inch piece of dictionary pages printed paper to Suffuse paper on front of card; adhere paper with window cutout to card so that dictionary print shows through open window.

5 *Embellish window opening:* Trim leaf motif from printed paper; adhere to dictionary pages paper inside window; outline with marker. Stamp black butterfly onto almanac pages paper; cut out and adhere inside window. Adhere crystals down butterfly's body. Print sentiment on label tape; adhere to layout in window.

6 Close window. Stamp black "Spring" and flourish on card front. ✳

Sources: Printed papers from Basic Grey (Season and Suffuse), Creative Imaginations and Scenic Route Paper Co.; stamps from Hero Arts (flourish) and Autumn Leaves; chalk stamp pads from Clearsnap Inc.; crystals from Mark Richards Inc.; Coluzzle template from Close to My Heart; label maker from DYMO.

Merci Triangle Card

DESIGN BY **LINDSEY BOTKIN**

Project Note

Adhere elements using paper adhesive unless instructed otherwise.

1 Vertically score a 10½ x 3½-inch strip of white card stock 3½ inches from both ends. Score each end panel from top left corner to bottom right corner (Fig. 1, page 174) and fold triangles to form 3½-inch-square card (Fig. 2, page 174).

2 Cut a 3¼-inch square of Celebrate paper; cut in half on the diagonal. Center and adhere paper triangles to card, centering them on card stock to leave even borders. Wrap ribbon around card, tying it in a bow at right edge.

3 Stamp brown flowers and stems onto a 2 x 2⅛-inch piece of white card stock off left edge. Center and adhere card stock to a 2¼ x 2⅜-inch piece of brown card stock; center on front of card over ribbon; adhere to upper left triangle only.

4 Stamp red flower on white card stock; cut out and adhere to stamped image using dimensional glue dot.

5 *Inside card:* Stamp brown flower stems on right side of a 2⅞-inch square of white card stock. Center and adhere card stock to a 3¼-inch square of Celebrate paper; center and adhere inside card. ❋

Sources: Card stock from Stampin' Up!; printed paper from My Mind's Eye; stamps from Inkadinkado; ribbon from May Arts.

Materials

Card stock: white, brown
Celebrate printed paper
Stamps: "merci," flowers
Ink: brown, red
½-inch-wide sheer white polka-dot ribbon
Dimensional glue dots
Paper adhesive

Owl Thank You

DESIGN BY **LINDSEY BOTKIN**

Materials
Card stock: white, bright pink
Buttercream Bliss double-sided printed
  paper
Stamps: Hooty, Thank You
Black ink
Markers: peachy yellow, tan, bright pink
½-inch-wide white cotton trim
3 copper eyelets
Punches: ⅛-inch hole, 2-inch circle,
  2½-inch scalloped circle
Paper adhesive

1 Horizontally score a 5½ x 8½-inch piece of white card stock 2¼ inches from top and 2½ inches from bottom. Fold bottom panel up and top panel down.

2 Punch three holes evenly spaced down center of a 5½ x 1-inch strip of Buttercream Bliss paper on yellow pin-dot side; attach eyelets. Adhere a strip of bright pink card stock to reverse side behind eyelets.

3 Cut a 5½ x 2⅞-inch piece of Buttercream Bliss paper with scallops along bottom edge; adhere strip with eyelets to paper ¼ inch from top edge. Adhere paper panel to top flap of card ⅛ inch from fold. Adhere lace trim to card between pin-dot strip and scalloped border.

4 Stamp owl onto white card stock; color with markers. Punch 2-inch circle around owl. Center and adhere owl circle to scalloped circle punched from bright pink card stock; center and adhere owl to top flap of card, overlapping bottom edge.

5 Stamp "Thank You" onto lower right corner of card.

6 *Inside card:* Center and adhere a 5½ x 1⅜-inch strip of bright pink card stock across top flap. Cover center panel with yellow pin-dot side of Buttercream Bliss paper; adhere a 5½ x 1½-inch strip of Buttercream Bliss paper with scalloped edge across pin-dot paper near bottom edge. Adhere a 3-inch-square of bright pink card stock to lower right corner, ⅛ inch from right and bottom edges. ✿

Sources: Printed paper from Sassafras Lass; stamps from Inkadinkado; Ciao markers from Copic; lace trim from Melissa Frances; punches from Uchida of America.

Have a Great Birthday

DESIGN BY **LINDSEY BOTKIN**

Project Note

Adhere elements using paper adhesive unless instructed otherwise.

1 Horizontally score a 4¼ x 10-inch strip of black card stock 2½ inches from top and 2½ inches from bottom. Fold bottom flap up and top flap down to meet in center.

2 Adhere printed paper to top and bottom panels, leaving even, narrow black borders. Adhere a 1¼-inch-wide strip of contrasting printed paper across top flap, ⅞ inch from fold. Tie ribbon around top flap over contrasting paper strip, knotting ends close to right edge.

3 Using black marker, draw a straight line across top panel of printed paper near top edge. Open card and lay flat; use piercing tool to make needle holes along line to give the appearance of stitching.

4 Stamp floral corner onto all corners of a 3-inch square of white card stock; distress card-stock edges. Adhere to black card stock; cut out, leaving narrow black borders.

5 Stamp clematis vine onto contrasting printed paper; punch out with circle punch and adhere to center of stamped white card stock. Stamp clematis again onto pink section of printed paper; cut out center flower and adhere to center of first stamped clematis image using a glue dot.

6 Adhere stamped square to upper flap over ribbon, ¼ inch from left and top edges.

7 Attach felt brad to bottom flap to slightly overlap stamped square and hold card closed. Stamp "Have a Great Birthday" onto lower right corner of bottom flap.

8 *Inside card:* Adhere printed paper to center panel leaving narrow black borders. Center and adhere a 2⅞ x 4-inch piece of white card stock

to printed paper. Using black marker, draw lines around printed paper near edge. Use piercing tool to make needle holes along lines. ✽

Materials

Card stock: white, black
Printed paper
Stamps: floral corner, clematis vine, "Have a Great Birthday"
Black solvent-based ink
Extra-fine-point black marker
½-inch-wide black sheer ribbon with white pin dots
Black felt brad
2-inch hole punch
Edge distresser
Paper piercer
Paper adhesive
Glue dot

Sources: Fleuriste Designer printed paper from Cosmo Cricket; stamps from Inkadinkado; solvent-based ink from Tsukineko Inc.; felt brad from Queen & Co.; circle punch from Uchida of America; edge distresser from Stampin' Up!

You're a Rockstar

DESIGN BY **LINDSEY BOTKIN**

1 Horizontally score a 4 x 10⅛-inch piece of gray card stock 4⅛ inches from top and 1⅛ inches from bottom.

2 Stamp small light blue stars onto light blue card stock; cut two pieces from stamped card stock, 1½ x 1¼ inches and 1½ x 4¼ inches.

3 Fold up bottom flap of card; adhere smaller stamped piece to flap ¼ inch from left edge. Staple across bottom fold to hold flap in upright position. Wrap ribbon around bottom flap; knot and trim ends.

4 Adhere Jack Die-Cut Star paper to top flap; trim edges even. Adhere remaining stamped piece to top flap ¼ inch from left edge.

5 Using Mega Scalloped Circle punch, punch circle from white card stock. Stamp large light green star onto another piece of white card stock; cut out. Stamp smaller black star outline onto solid blue paper; cut out. Stamp light blue stars reversed background onto scrap card stock; without re-inking stamp, stamp image again onto another piece of white card stock; over-stamp with black "You're a Rockstar" and trim oval around words.

6 Referring to photo, adhere scalloped circle to card ⅜ inch from top fold; layer stamped stars and "You're a Rockstar" as shown; adhere. Punch a ¹⁄₁₆-inch hole through smaller clear star and card; attach star with mini brad.

7 *Inside card:* Adhere a 4-inch square of Jack Die-cut Stars paper inside card, tucking bottom edge behind bottom flap. Center and adhere a 3½ x 2¾-inch piece of white card stock to printed paper. Attach larger clear star to upper left-hand quadrant with mini brad. ❋

Sources: Printed paper from Making Memories; stamp sets from Verve Visual; solvent-based ink from Tsukineko Inc.; clear stars from Heidi Swapp/Advantus Corp.; scalloped circle punch from Uchida of America.

Materials

Card stock: gray, light blue, white
Printed paper: Jack Die-cut Star, solid blue
Clear stamp sets: Polka Stars, Starlight Starbright, Seeing Stars
Ink: black solvent-based, light green, light blue
⅜-inch-wide green-and-white striped ribbon
Clear stars: 1-inch, 2⅛-inch
2 silver mini brads
Punches: ¹⁄₁₆-inch hole, Mega Scalloped Circle
Stapler with staples
Paper adhesive

Home Sweet Home

DESIGN BY **KELLY ANNE GRUNDHAUSER**

1 Vertically score an 11 x 5-inch piece of kraft card stock 4½ inches from left edge and 1¾ inches from right edge.

2 *Left Flap:* Adhere a 4½ x 1⅝-inch piece of Bernice paper to card with top and side edges even. Tear ½ inch off right edge of a 5 x 2½-inch piece of Wallflower paper; adhere to bottom of card.

3 Stamp black house with cloud, brown tree and brown "Home Sweet Home" on a 3⅜-inch square of kraft paper. Color image with markers; add details with glitter pens and white gel pen.

4 Wrap ribbon around coaster; knot on right edge and trim ends. Center and adhere stamped, colored image from step 3 to coaster; adhere coaster to left flap.

5 *Right flap:* Center and adhere a 1½ x 2¾-inch piece of Wallflower paper to flap near bottom. Tear right edge off a 2 x 1⅝-inch piece of Bernice paper; adhere to top of flap.

6 *Inside card:* Stamp "My Home" information panel inside card; color with markers and embellish with white gel pen. ✳

Sources: Printed paper from Graphic 45 (Wallflower) and Melissa Frances (Bernice); stamps from October Afternoon; distress ink and white pen from Ranger Industries; markers and glitter pens from Copic; ribbon from Making Memories; Zip Dry paper glue from Beacon Adhesives Inc.

Materials
Kraft card stock
Printed papers: Bernice, Wallflower double-sided
Stamps: tree with leaves, house, "Home Sweet Home," "My Home" information
Ink: brown distress, black
Markers
Glitter pens
White gel pen
1-inch-wide light green shirred fabric ribbon
3¾-inch-square cork coaster
Instant-dry paper glue

With Love Card

DESIGN BY **KELLY ANNE GRUNDHAUSER**

1 Cut a 12 x 5¼-inch piece of flower garden printed paper with solid brown base along bottom; punch top edge with threading water border punch.

2 Score and fold printed paper vertically 5½ inches from left edge and 1 inch from right edge. Fold left and right panels to center.

3 Cut a 6½ x 1-inch strip of pin-dot printed paper; cut 1 inch from one end and reserve. Adhere longer strip across bottom of left panel ⅜ inch from edge. Adhere shorter piece to matching position on right panel.

4 *Closure strip:* Cut an 11 x 1¹⁄₁₆-inch strip of the flowers printed paper; trim one end to a point. Wrap strip around card so that it is centered over pin-dot strip on front; adhere floral strip to back of card and to right flap only on front.

5 Stamp "with love" on scalloped tag; center over pin-dot strip on left panel ½ inch from fold. Adhere tag to card only along very top and bottom edges, leaving center of tag open so that floral strip can be threaded under tag to hold card closed. ✳

Sources: Printed papers from Heidi Grace Designs; tag from Jenny Bowlin Studio; stamp from Inque Boutique Stamps; threading water punch from Fiskars; Zip Dry paper glue from Beacon Adhesives Inc.

Mushroom Lighthouse Card

DESIGN BY **TAMI MAYBERRY**

1 Vertically score smooth side of an 8½ x 5½-inch piece of dark blue card stock 2⅛ inches from left edge and 2⅛ inches from right edge. Fold flaps toward center.

2 Cut a 4 x 5¼-inch piece of plaid paper. Slice in half down center and adhere halves to flaps, matching edges along center.

3 Center card over ribbon; adhere ribbon to back of card and to right flap only.

4 Stamp lighthouse onto natural card stock; color with colored pencils. Trim around image, centering it in a 2⅛ x 4¼-inch rectangle. Adhere lighthouse to red card stock and trim, leaving ⅛-inch borders. Adhere to dark blue card stock and trim, leaving ⅛-inch edges.

5 Close card; lay ribbon strands off to left of card. Position stamped image on card ¼ inch from right fold and ⅜ inch from top; adhere image to right flap only. Tie ribbon ends in a bow to hold card closed. ✸

Sources: Card stock from Prism Papers; printed paper from Scenic Route Paper Co.; rubber stamp from Cornish Heritage Farms.

FABULOUS FOLDS FOR CARD MAKING

Materials

Card stock: dark blue ridged, dark red, natural
Light blue plaid printed paper
3¾ x 1¾-inch lighthouse stamp
Black ink pad
Colored pencils
¼-inch-wide red-and-white gingham-checked ribbon
Craft knife
Paper adhesive

My Friend Card

DESIGN BY **KATHLEEN PANEITZ**

Materials

Pale pink card stock
Chelsea's Place journaling tags: paisley, polka-dot
Rub-on transfers: Chelsea's Place, Sentiments 2
⅜-inch-wide beige ribbon with white dots
Jumbo pebble brads: pink, light blue
Punches: ⅛-inch hole, corner rounder
Adhesive dots
Paper adhesive

Project Note
Adhere elements using paper adhesive unless instructed otherwise.

1 Use corner rounder punch to round off corners on a 5½ x 4½-inch piece of pink card stock. Center and adhere pink checked rub-on transfer with red border and flowers to card ⅛ inch from top.

2 Tie ribbon in a bow; trim ends and adhere to card ½ inch from top using an adhesive dot.

3 With pointed end at left, embellish journaling area of polka-dot tag with "Thank you so much" and red flower rub-on transfers. With pointed end at right, embellish journaling area of paisley tag with "my friend" and paisley motif rub-on transfers.

4 Punch a ⅛-inch hole ⅜ inch from left edge of card and 1½ inches from bottom; attach polka-dot tag with pink brad. Punch matching hole on right edge of card; attach paisley tag with blue brad. ✳

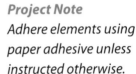

Sources: Journaling tags, rub-on transfers and pebble brads from Making Memories; "Thank you so much" rub-on transfer from Scenic Route Paper Co.; ribbon from May Arts.

Happy Day! Gatefold Card

DESIGN BY **KATHLEEN PANEITZ**

FABULOUS FOLDS FOR CARD MAKING

Materials
Card stock: light blue (optional), cream
Printed paper: Piccadilly, cream notebook print
4-inch flower die cuts: blue lined notebook print, white with brown and blue circles
Black rub-on transfers: Whoa Nelly medium black letters Sentiments Set 2
3¼-inch-wide brown grosgrain ribbon
Punches: 1½-inch circle, corner rounder
Transparent photo-fastener tabs
Adhesive dots
Paper adhesive

Project Note
Adhere elements using paper adhesive unless instructed otherwise.

1 Round off corners on a 5-inch square of Piccadilly paper and a 4¾ x 4-inch piece of cream notebook printed paper using corner rounder punch. Center and adhere notebook printed paper to Piccadilly paper ¾ inch from top. Center and adhere "to you!" rub-on transfer to notebook paper.

2 Attach right edge of blue flower die cut to card with a photo-fastener tab so that die cut's right edge is even with edge of notebook paper. In same manner, attach polka-dot flower die cut to left side of card.

3 Adhere "happy day" rub-on transfer to light blue reverse side of a piece of Piccadilly paper. **Option:** *Adhere rub-on transfer to light blue card stock. Adhere "smile"/bird rub-on transfer to cream card stock. Punch out transfers using 1½-inch circle punch; adhere blue circle to polka-dot flower and cream circle to blue flower.*

4 Tie ribbon in a bow; adhere to blue flower above circle using glue dot. ✱

Sources: Tudor printed paper from KaiserCraft; notebook printed paper from Steel Toed Mary Jane Collection by Prima Marketing; die cuts from Creative Café; rub-on transfers from Luxe Designs (letters) and Scenic Route Paper Co.; punches from EK Success Ltd.; Flip Flop fasteners from Boxer Scrapbook Productions.

Crosshatch Purse Card

DESIGN BY **KERI LEE SEREIKA**

Materials

Card stock: intense pink, white
Dottie Ann pink paper mesh
Biased Stripe Backgrounder rubber
   stamp
Chalk inks: lime, rose
⅜-inch-wide light green grosgrain ribbon
   with white pin dots
2 (¾-inch) pink flowers with green leaves
2 bright green micro mini brads
Paper piercer
Paper adhesive

1 Horizontally score a 5½ x 8½ inch piece of rose card stock 1 inch from top and 3½ inches from bottom. Fold bottom flap up and top flap down.

2 Mark top fold 1 inch from each side edge. Cut through all layers from mark to bottom corner (Fig. 1, page 174).

3 Use lime ink to stamp background lines onto a 4¼ x 5½-inch piece of white card stock; re-ink stamp and apply again, offsetting lines slightly. Clean stamp; turn stamp a quarter turn and stamp lines using rose ink. Re-ink stamp and apply again, off-setting lines.

4 Adhere stamped card stock to bottom flap; trim edges even. Center and adhere a 1¹⁄₁₆-inch-wide strip of paper mesh across top flap; trim ends even.

5 *Purse handle:* Open "purse," leaving top flap folded down. Poke a hole though flap and back of card near top right and left corners. Attach a sheer blossom and leaf and one end of ribbon to card with brad. Repeat on other side. ✱

Sources: Card stock from Prism Papers; paper mesh from Magic Mesh; stamp from Cornish Heritage Farms; chalk inks from Clearsnap Inc.; sheer blossoms and leaves and brads from Creative Impressions.

Thinking About You Pocket Card

DESIGN BY **KERI LEE SEREIKA**

FABULOUS FOLDS FOR CARD MAKING

Materials

Card stock: intense pink, black, white
Sugar pink/cream/green striped printed paper
Stamp sets: Spring Blooms, Punchy Words
Chalk inks: lime, rose, black
14 inches ½-inch-wide lime swirls sheer organdy ribbon
2 pink mini brads
Die cutter
Dies: Small Classic Oval (#S4 112), Small Classic Scalloped Oval (#SF 113)
Spray bottle filled with rubbing alcohol
Paper adhesive

1 Horizontally score a 5½ x 10½ inch piece of pink card stock 2 inches from top and 4½ inches from bottom. Fold bottom flap up and top flap down.

2 Wrap ribbon around a 5¼ x 1¾-inch piece of striped printed paper ¼ inch from bottom, knotting ends on front near right edge. Center and adhere printed paper to top flap.

3 Ink bloom portion of rose stamp with rose ink and stems and leaves with lime ink; stamp onto white card stock. Spray stamped image with alcohol to soften edges.

4 Punch oval with stamped rose in center; center and adhere to scalloped oval punched from black card stock. Adhere ovals to top flap ⅜ inch from top and ½ inch from left edge.

5 Open top flap, leaving bottom flap folded up. Poke a hole though flap and back of card near top right and left corners. Attach mini brads.

6 Stamp black "thinking about you" on lower right corner of card.

7 Ink bloom portion of rose stamp with rose ink and stem and leaves with lime ink; stamp onto left side of a 5 x 3¾-inch piece of white card stock. Tuck card into pocket. ❋

Sources: Card stock from Prism Papers; printed paper from Memory Box; stamp sets from Gina K Designs; chalk inks from Clearsnap Inc.; dies and die cutter from Spellbinders Paper Arts.

Thoughts of You

DESIGN BY **KERI LEE SEREIKA**

1 Horizontally score a 4¼ x 11-inch piece of cream card stock 3½ inches from top and 2 inches from bottom. Fold bottom flap up and top flap down so edges meet.

2 Open card and lay flat, right side up, with top flap at bottom. Stamp flowers on top flap, stamping them off bottom edge. Ink stamp with light brown ink and stamp onto scrap card stock. Without re-inking stamp, stamp image onto card. Repeat twice. Ink a different stamp with light brown ink and stamp onto card over lighter images; repeat. Ink a different stamp with dark brown ink; stamp twice up left side of card over lighter images.

3 Stamp dark brown "Thoughts of You" in upper right corner of top flap.

4 Pierce two scalloped rows of holes on bottom flap ¼ inch from fold.

5 *Closure strip:* Cut a 10 x 1½-inch strip of dark brown card stock; wrap around card, overlapping ends on back and adhering ends to each other where they overlap. Cut a 4¼ x 1¼-inch piece of printed paper; center and adhere to brown strip on front of card. Position strip over seam between flaps to hold card closed. ❋

Sources: Card stock from Prism Papers; printed paper from Webster's Pages; stamp sets from Cornish Heritage Farms; chalk inks from Clearsnap Inc.

Materials

Card stock: cream, brown
Coco Fresh Baked printed paper
Stamp sets: Silhouette Blooms I and II
Chalk inks: light brown, dark brown
Scalloped paper-piercing template
Paper piercer
Paper adhesive

Forever Friends

DESIGN BY **LISA SILVER**

Materials

Card stock: cream, rust
Island printed paper
Stamp sets: Script Essential Expressions,
    Friend Centers
Wild rose rubber stamp
Ink: rust dye, sepia, walnut distress
1-inch-wide rust satin ribbon
3 complementary buttons
Watercolor brush
Ink-blending tool
Die cutter
Dies: Large Classic Ovals (#S4 110), Large
    Classic Scalloped Ovals (#S4 111),
    Large Classic Scalloped Rectangles
    (#S4 133)
Adhesive dots
Paper adhesive

Project Note

Adhere elements using paper adhesive unless instructed otherwise.

1 Vertically score an 8½ x 5½-inch piece of printed paper 2⅛ inches from left edge and 2⅛ inches from right edge; fold flaps to meet in center. Ink edges and folds sepia and brown, blending colors with blending tool.

2 Adhere ribbon horizontally across left flap 2¼ inches from top.

3 Die-cut and emboss a 3⅝ x 2¾-inch oval of cream card stock. Ink edges sepia and brown, blending colors with blending tool.

4 Using rust dye ink, stamp wild rose at an angle onto oval; watercolor image with diluted rust dye and sepia distress inks. Stamp dark brown "forever friends" over image toward right edge.

5 Die-cut and emboss a 4 x 3⅛-inch scalloped oval of rust card stock. Center and adhere stamped image to rust scalloped oval; adhere to left flap only.

6 Adhere buttons to right flap using adhesive dots, positioning largest button so that it slightly overlaps edge of rust oval and serves as closure.

7 *Inside card:* Die-cut and emboss a 3⅛ x 4-inch scalloped rectangle of cream card stock; ink edges sepia and brown, blending colors with blending tool. Stamp sentiment in brown; adhere rectangle to card. ✽

Sources: *Printed paper by Crate Paper; stamps from Cornish Heritage Farms; inks from Ranger Industries; dies and die cutter from Spellbinders Paper Arts.*

Glittered Floral Surprise

DESIGN BY **DIANE W. TUGGLE**

Project Notes

Adhere elements using paper adhesive unless instructed otherwise.

Vertically score a 12 x 4-inch piece of pink card stock 4 inches from left edge and 4 inches from right edge. Fold in right flap (center flap), then left flap (front flap).

Materials

Card stock: textured light pink, white, black
Black-and-white polka-dot printed paper
2-inch pink paper flower
⅓ of a 3-inch pad of pink sticky notes
Stamp sets: Endless Love, Soul Mates Word Puzzle
Ink pads: black, pink
Pink fine-tip marker
Embossing pen
Liquid epoxy coating
½-inch acrylic circle
25 inches ⅜-inch-wide pink grosgrain ribbon
Fine iridescent glitter
Glue dot
Adhesive foam dot
Paper adhesive

Front Flap

1 Cut a 3¾-inch square of black card stock, a 3½-inch square of white card stock and a 3-inch square of polka-dot printed paper. Cut squares in half on the diagonal; center and adhere triangles to one another in two matching layered sets. Adhere layered triangles to upper right and lower left corners of card, leaving even borders around edges and between the two triangles.

2 Lay ribbon across front of card so that 8 inches extend past right edge; adhere ribbon to front of card using a glue dot.

3 Stamp black large floral motif onto white card stock. Color narrow inner scalloped border and circles along edge with pink marker. Fill pink circles with liquid epoxy; sprinkle with glitter and let dry for a few minutes.

4 Color over black scalloped border using embossing pen; immediately sprinkle with glitter, then tap off excess.

5 Cut out stamped image. Adhere paper flower to center using liquid epoxy.

6 Stamp black small flower onto white card stock. Color center circle with pink marker; cut out and adhere to paper flower with adhesive dot. Adhere acrylic circle over stamped flower center.

7 Center and adhere floral motif to card.

Center Flap

1 Stamp black "My love for you …" sentiment onto center of a 3⅝-inch square of white card stock. Lightly over-stamp with pink circle motif; ink edges of card stock pink.

2 Center and adhere stamped square to a 3⅞-inch square of black card stock; center and adhere to center flap.

Inside Card

1 Stamp side panels of card interior with black "Best Friends," "side by side" and flourishes.

2 Center and adhere sticky notes to a 3¼-inch square of black card stock; center and adhere to center of card's interior. ✹

Source: Card stock, printed paper, stamps, ink pad, marker, embossing pen, Liquid Glass liquid epoxy, Prisma glitter, acrylic circle and 3-D Foam Dot from Close To My Heart.

IRIS
FOLDING

Carefully placed strips of folded paper create the focal point on these stunning cards. Start with one of these easy-to-follow patterns and soon you'll be on your way to discovering how easy it is to create original designs of your own!

Like many paper crafts, iris folding has made its way across the globe, where enthusiasts in Holland and Japan have created many innovative designs. And like many paper crafts, this is one that looks more difficult than it is!

The results are impressive, but the technique involves only two simple steps: folding strips of lightweight paper in half, and gluing or taping the strips in place, one at a time in numerical order, following a pattern template.

When the strips are in place and the final accent is added to fill the last little open space, after a bit of snipping to neaten it from the back, the card front is done.

The window opening in which the design is worked is called the aperture. In a camera lens, the aperture opens and closes, always a circle. For iris folding, however, the aperture can be circular, oval, square, triangular or another geometric shape, or a heart, Christmas tree, bird, sailboat, teapot, flower or other simple shape.

Like strip piecing and log cabin quilting—fabric techniques that iris folding resembles—you can use scraps left from other projects or purchase supplies for a particular project. Iris folding is a wonderful way to recycle gift wrap or the linings of envelopes, but it's also an excellent excuse to shop for special papers. Projects only require small amounts, so even the most expensive paper goes a long way.

If you own rubber stamps, you can create your own unique papers, too. You can incorporate prints, stripes and solid colors—whatever the pattern calls for or whatever you think looks good together. Iris folding allows for a lot of individuality; no two people will have the same collection of papers.

Getting Started

Once strips are cut, the next step is to fold the lightweight paper strips in half lengthwise.

Iris Folding 2, **published by Search Press.**

This part of the process is portable, an easy thing to do while waiting for a doctor's appointment or sitting at the airport. Many people like to fold strips ahead of time, organizing them by color, so there are plenty on hand.

You can substitute pieces of ribbon or strips of heavier paper and card stock, in which case no folding will be needed.

Though you can fold strips to the precise measurements for a given pattern, it's easier to fold long strips to cut as needed, even if it means having leftovers.

Making a Card with an Aperture

The front of an iris fold card is always lined, hiding the "messy" part of the folded strips. Project instructions will explain where to cut, score and fold the card, as well as how to cut the aperture opening.

For best results, use a craft knife, a ruler, if needed, and a cutting mat so the edges of the aperture are smooth.

To change the size of the card, enlarge or reduce the aperture opening as well as the pattern template, and adjust the width of the strips to suit the new size.

one strip at a time. Follow the color progression spelled out in the instructions, and refer to the photo if you get confused.

The last piece is often velvet, holographic paper, metallic paper or a special snippet of memorabilia.

Remember: You are adding strips to the back of the aperture, starting at the outer edges and working toward the center of the iris to build the pattern.

Remove the tape that was holding the card over the template. Look at the card front to make sure no paper strips or tape are showing where they shouldn't, and tidy up the wrong side of the card front if needed before securing the lining.

Beyond the Basics

Iris fold cards can be simple and elegant, nothing more than a shaped opening with beautiful strips of paper forming the iris inside the aperture. Or you can embellish your cards with stickers, die-cut shapes, silk flowers, feathers, gems, beads and other dimensional accents—whatever you want. ✳

Iris-fold rubber stamps from Stamp N Plus Scrap N

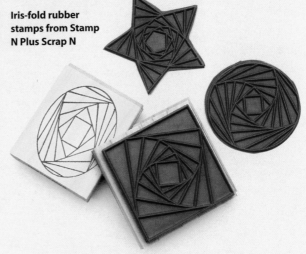

Adding the Strips

Trace or photocopy the pattern. Use temporary (low-tack) tape to tape the pattern template to a cutting mat or other work surface. Tape the card with aperture right side down over the pattern. Following the numbers, lay paper strips in position, right side down, along the guidelines. Cut off excess and secure strips with double-faced tape,

Iris-Folded Blossom

DESIGN BY **JULIE EBERSOLE**

1 Form a 5½ x 4¼-inch top-folded card from apricot card stock.

2 Referring to photo throughout, wrap striped ribbon around front panel of card 1½ inches from bottom; knot ends on front near right edge, securing a 2-inch piece of orange ribbon in knot. Trim all ribbon ends at an angle.

3 Cut a 4¼ x 3¼-inch piece of celery card stock; punch flower from center. Center and adhere card stock right side down over iris-folding pattern using removable tape.

Iris Folding

1 Cut two 12 x 1-inch strips from each of the printed papers; fold strips in half, wrong sides facing, to form 12 x ½-inch strips. Using glue stick, glue strips closed.

2 Working in order according to numbers on pattern, adhere strips to reverse side of punched card stock using glue stick, aligning folded edges of strips with lines on pattern and trimming strips as needed.

3 Remove pattern and trim any ends of strips that extend beyond edges of card stock. Secure strips as needed with adhesive tape.

Finishing

1 Flip celery green card stock right side up; attach mini brads in corners.

2 Cut a 4½ x 3½-inch piece of white card stock. Center and adhere iris-folded panel to white card stock using strips of foam mounting tape to maintain an even surface.

3 Punch 12–14 (⅝-inch) circles from white card stock. Using glue stick, adhere circles to

Materials
Card stock: celery green, apricot, white
Printed paper: Old Olive, Pumpkin Pie, Taken with Teal
1⅛-inch orange mulberry-paper flower
Brads: 4 orange mini, ⁵⁄₁₆-inch light blue crystal
Ribbon: ⅜-inch-wide celery-and-white stripe, ⅝-inch-wide shimmery orange
Punches: ⅝-inch circle, Giga Flower
Triangular iris-folding diagram
Foam mounting tape
Tape: adhesive, double-sided, removable
Glue stick

reverse side of white card stock along bottom and right edges to create "scalloped edges."

4 Using double-sided tape, adhere white panel to card front ³⁄₁₆ inch from top and left edges. Attach crystal brad to paper flower; using foam mounting tape, adhere flower to center of iris-folded design. ✱

Sources: Printed papers from Stampin' Up!; paper flower from Prima Marketing; ribbons from May Arts; Giga Flower punch from Marvy Uchida; iris-folding diagram from www.cardsandcrafts.freeservers.com.

Enjoy Your Day

DESIGN BY **LISA SILVER**

Materials

Card stock: bright white, yellow, light pink, white
Two Scoops printed papers: Crème Brulee, Dreamsicle
Stamps: Kim Hughes Bloomin' Beautiful stamp set; Tyson the Turtle stamp
Black dye ink
Markers
3-dimensional black gel pen
Glitter pens
Piercing tool
Corner rounder
Dimensional foam tape
Instant-dry paper glue

Project Note

Adhere elements using instant-dry paper glue unless instructed otherwise.

1 Form a 4¼ x 4¼-inch top-folded card from pink card stock.

2 Cut a 4 x 4-inch piece of Crème Brulee printed paper.

3 Referring to photo throughout, stamp turtle onto Crème Brulee printed paper square, positioning turtle ¾ inch from bottom edge and ⅞ inch from right edge. Highlight turtle's eyes with white pigment pen; darken centers with black gel pen. Add shadow under turtle using light gray marker.

4 Stamp "take time to enjoy your day" sentiment onto Crème Brulee printed paper above turtle.

Iris Folding

1 Trim out turtle's shell, cutting just inside stamped lines.

2 Cut 1-inch-wide strips of yellow, pink and white card stock. **Note:** *The iris-folding strips are not folded in half for this design.*

3 Adhere strips to reverse side of turtle shell cutout, arranging and overlapping pieces as desired.

4 Trim any ends of strips that extend beyond edges of card stock.

Finishing

1 Cut a 1 x 4-inch strip of yellow card stock. Remove guide from corner rounder and punch scallops along one long edge. Pierce a hole in each scallop; highlight holes with glitter pens. Adhere scalloped strip to iris-folded panel ¼ inch from left edge.

2 Cut a ¾ x 4-inch strip from Dreamsicle printed paper; adhere to scalloped strip ¹⁄₁₆ inch from right edge.

3 Center and adhere iris-folded panel to card front using dimensional foam tape.

4 Stamp small and medium flowers onto bright white card stock; color with markers and embellish with glitter pens. Cut out flowers and adhere to card as shown using dimensional foam tape. ✳

Sources: Bright white card stock from Neenah Paper Inc.; printed papers from BasicGrey; stamp set and stamp from Cornish Heritage Farms; Copic markers; Spica glitter pens; black glaze pen from Sakura; Zip Dry Paper Glue from Beacon Adhesives Inc.

Simplicity

DESIGN BY **SHARON M. REINHART**

1 Cut brown card stock 5½ x 11 inches. Score horizontally 4¼ and 8½ inches from top to form top-folded card base with a bottom flap that serves as easel.

2 Cut a 5⅛ x 4-inch piece of Bohemia printed card stock; center and adhere to card front.

3 Cut a 4⅞ x 3¾-inch piece of brown card stock. Center and punch a 1⅞-inch square in card stock ¾ inch from top edge.

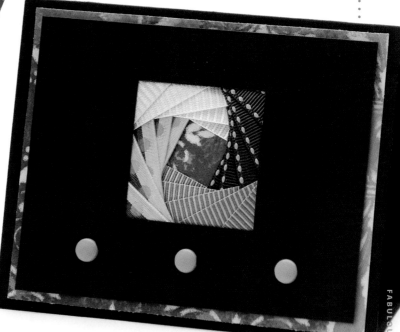

Iris Folding

1 Center and stamp square iris-folding pattern on a 4¼-inch square of white card stock; this will serve as pattern.

2 Position brown card stock right side down with pattern centered in opening; adhere with low-tack or removable tape.

3 Cut two 12-inch strips from each of the four ribbons.

4 Referring to photo throughout, plan layout of ribbons. Position ribbon A on reverse side of square in lower right corner, aligning edge of ribbon slightly below line on pattern. ***Note:*** *Because you will be using ⅜-inch-wide ribbons on a pattern designed for ½-inch-wide strips, all ribbons should be placed slightly below their respective pattern lines. Adhere one end of ribbon to card stock; trim excess and adhere at opposite end.*

5 In the same manner, adhere ribbon B in upper right corner, ribbon C in upper left corner and ribbon D in lower left corner. Continue until all areas are filled except center square.

6 Remove low-tack or removable tape.

Materials

Card stock: brown, white
Bohemia printed card stock
Iris-folding square pattern rubber stamp
Black or brown ink pad
3 pink brads
Dashes, Dots and Checks ⅜-inch-wide
   complementary printed ribbons:
   white-on-white, brown with pink
   stitching, brown/pink dots, pink/
   mauve stripes
Punches: ⅛-inch hole, 1⅞-inch square
Tape: cellophane, double-sided, low-tack
   or removable
Foam mounting tape
Glue stick

Finishing

1 Center and punch three evenly spaced ⅛-inch holes across bottom of iris-folded frame as shown; attach brads.

2 Center and adhere iris-folded panel to card front using adhesive foam tape. ✱

Sources: Printed card stock from My Mind's Eye; rubber stamp from Stamp N Plus Scrap N; ribbon from Michaels Stores Inc.; square punch from McGill.

Blooming Thank You

DESIGN BY **KATHLEEN PANEITZ**

1 Form a 5 x 4½-inch top-folded card from light blue card stock.

2 Referring to photo throughout, adhere die-cut flower petals to white card stock. Trim around outer edges, leaving ⅛-inch border around flower. Center and cut a 2¼-inch circle from flower center.

3 Outline center circle and die-cut petals using fine-tip marker.

Iris Folding

1 Cut four 2 x 1-inch strips from each side of each of the printed papers; fold in half, wrong sides facing, to form 2 x ½-inch strips.

2 Referring to photo throughout, adhere four folded strips to reverse side of flower center, working clockwise and adhering one strip of each color in the first layer. Keeping the same color order, adhere strips for the second layer across the corners formed by the first layer. Repeat to add two more layers, leaving a small open square in center.

Finishing

1 Center and adhere flower panel to card front.

2 Leaving card's top fold intact, trim light blue card stock around flower, leaving a ¼-inch-wide border of light blue.

3 Using fine-tip marker, add evenly spaced dots to light blue border.

4 Attach pebble brad to card front through flower center.

5 Apply "thank you" rub-on transfer to bottom right flower petal. ❃

Sources: Printed papers from Crate Paper; die cut from Creative Imaginations; rub-on transfer from Scenic Route Paper Co.; pebble brad and circle cutter from Making Memories.

Materials

Card stock: light blue, white
Double-sided printed paper: Grass, Breeze
Flower die cut
⅜-inch black "thank you" rub-on transfer
Black fine-tip marker
Decorative ⅝-inch light green-and-white pebble brad
Circle cutter
Paper adhesive

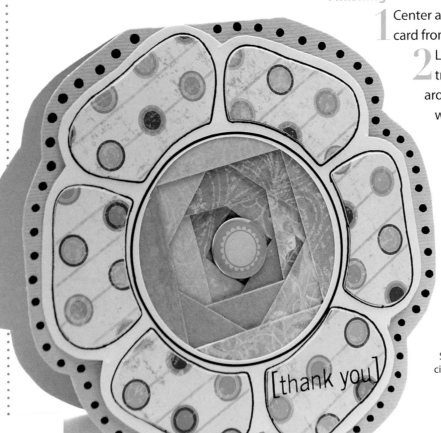

[thank you]

Lucky You

DESIGN BY **KELLY ANNE GRUNDHAUSER**

Project Note

Adhere elements using instant-dry paper glue unless instructed otherwise.

1 Form a 5 x 6-inch top-folded card from Mantis printed card stock.

2 Cut another 5 x 6-inch piece of Mantis printed card stock for iris-folded panel. Using pattern on page 171 and referring to photo throughout, center and cut shamrock from card stock, positioning cutout ⅜ inch from bottom edge.

Iris Folding

1 Cut three 1½-inch-wide strips from each of the four printed papers, cutting the length of the paper sheet; fold strips in half, wrong sides facing, to form ¾-inch-wide strips.

2 Turn panel with cutout wrong side up. Referring to photo throughout, adhere first strip of color A across bottom of opening (shamrock stem) at a slight angle, about ½ inch from edge with folded edge toward center. **Note:** *Adhere strip from one end of folded strip; cut and use the same strip to add following strips until it is used up.*

3 In the same manner, add three more strips of color A, applying each at a slight angle as shown; the fourth strip will cover the bottom edges of the bottom shamrock leaves.

4 Adhere the first strip of color B up the left edge of the shamrock; the first strip of color C across the top; and the first strip of color D down the right edge. Add the second strip of color A across the bottom.

5 Continue working around shamrock, adding strips in order, overlapping strips and fanning them out at angles of 15–30 degrees as desired to keep pattern even and consistent.

Materials

Mantis printed card stock
Dark green solid card stock or paper
4 complementary green printed papers
Small tag
Sentiment stamp
Black ink
Fine jute twine
Lucky horseshoe charm
Double-sided tape
Instant-dry paper glue

6 Continue adding strips in order until only a small open square—about ½ inch—remains in center. Adhere plain green paper to reverse side of design to cover center.

Finishing

1 Wrap fine jute twine around iris-folded design near top as shown; adhere ends on reverse side.

2 Adhere iris-folded design to card front using double-sided tape.

3 Stamp sentiment on tag; tie tag and charm to card as shown. ✻

Sources: All in the Family printed card stock from Core'dinations; printed papers from K&Company and SEI; tag from Making Memories; Zip Dry Paper Glue from Beacon Adhesives Inc.

Time to Celebrate

DESIGN BY **KELLY ANNE GRUNDHAUSER**

Time to *Celebrate!*

Project Note

Adhere elements using instant-dry paper glue unless instructed otherwise.

1 Form a 4 x 8-inch side-folded card from Mermaid card stock with mermaid side facing out.

2 Cut a 3¾ x 7¾-inch piece from Mermaid card stock for iris-folded panel.

3 Score both pieces of card stock on the black side in a ½-inch grid pattern; sand lightly to reveal the mermaid lines beneath. Set the card aside.

4 Using pattern on page 171 and referring to photo throughout, cut balloon from sanded card stock, positioning cutout ½ inch from top edge.

Iris Folding

1 Cut two or three 1½-inch-wide strips from each of the three printed papers, cutting the length of the paper sheet; fold strips in half, wrong sides facing, to create ¾-inch-wide strips.

2 Turn panel with cutout wrong side up. Referring to the photo throughout, adhere first strip of color A along left side of balloon about ½ inch from edge with folded edge toward center.

Note: *Adhere strip from one end of folded strip; cut and use the same strip to add following strips until it is used up.*

3 In the same manner, adhere the first strip of color B up the right edge of the balloon, and the first strip of color C across the top.

4 Continue working around balloon, adding strips in order, overlapping strips and fanning them out at angles of 15–30 degrees as desired to keep pattern even and consistent.

Materials

Mermaid color-core card stock
Simply Luxe dotted printed papers: pink, lime, blue
"Celebrate" sentiment stamp
Black chalk ink
6 inches ½-inch-wide lime twill tape
3 small white buttons
Scoring tool
Sandpaper
Double-sided tape
Instant-dry paper glue

5 Continue adding strips in order until only a small opening remains in center. Adhere printed paper right side down to reverse side of design to cover center.

Finishing

1 Center and adhere iris-folded panel to card front using double-sided tape.

2 Adhere twill tape to card front for balloon "string" using double-sided tape.

3 Stamp sentiment onto ½ x 3½-inch strip of green printed paper; adhere to red printed paper and trim, leaving narrow borders. Adhere sentiment to card near bottom, overhanging right edge as shown.

4 Adhere buttons to left end of sentiment as shown.

5 Embellish interior of card with strips of printed paper and additional stamped sentiments as desired. ✱

Sources: Black Magic card stock from Core'dinations; printed papers from Luxe Designs; twill tape from Creative Imaginations; Zip Dry Paper Glue from Beacon Adhesives Inc.

You're Sweet

DESIGN BY **LISA SILVER**

Materials

Card stock: bright white, white, dark red, black
Kim Hughes Sweet Thang stamp set
Dye inks: gray, black
12 inches ⁷⁄₁₆-inch-wide sheer black/white pin-dot ribbon
Corner rounder
Paper punches: ⅛-inch hole, 1-inch circle punch
Die cutter
Classic Scalloped Rectangle dies (#S4 133)
Foam mounting tape
Instant-dry paper glue

Iris Folding

1. Referring to photo throughout, stamp gray lollipop onto center of white scalloped rectangle. Stamp black "sugar" next to lollipop stick as shown.

2. Using 1-inch circle punch, punch out interior of lollipop; lay lollipop panel right side down.

3. Cut 1-inch-wide strips of dark red and white card stock. **Note:** *The iris-folding strips are not folded in half for this design.*

4. Referring to photo throughout, adhere strips to reverse side of lollipop cutout, arranging and overlapping pieces as desired.

5. Trim any ends of strips that extend beyond edges of card stock.

Project Note

Adhere elements using instant-dry paper glue unless instructed otherwise.

1. Form a 4¼ x 5½-inch top-folded card from white card stock.

2. Die-cut a 3⅝ x 2⅜-inch scalloped rectangle from bright white card stock using die cutter and die. Cut a 2⅞ x 3¹¹⁄₁₆-inch rectangle from dark red card stock; center and adhere scalloped rectangle to dark red rectangle.

Finishing

1. Remove guide from corner rounder and punch scallops across bottom of card front. Punch a ⅛-inch hole in each scallop.

2. Tie ribbon around card front as shown; knot close to left edge. Trim notches in ribbon ends.

3. Center and adhere lollipop panel to card front. ✹

Sources: Bright white card stock from Neenah Paper Inc.; stamp set from Cornish Heritage Farms; corner rounder from EK Success Ltd.; die cutter and Nestabilities dies from Spellbinder Paper Arts; Zip Dry Paper Glue from Beacon Adhesives Inc.

America the Beautiful

DESIGN BY **LISA SILVER**

Project Note

Adhere elements using instant-dry paper glue unless instructed otherwise.

1 Form a 5½ x 4¼-inch top-folded card from white card stock.

2 Cut a 5¼ x 4-inch piece of dark blue card stock.

3 Turn card stock wrong side up. Stamp Supah Star onto card stock ⅝ inch from top edge and ½ inch from right edge; cut out star just inside stamped outline.

4 Turn card stock over. Referring to photo throughout, adhere ¾-inch wide strips of white card stock and a 1¼-inch strip of red card stock to dark blue card stock, edge to edge; trim ends even with star outline and right edge of card stock.

5 Using zigzag stitch, machine-stitch over edges of red and white card-stock strips.

Iris Folding

1 Cut 1-inch-wide strips of white card stock and Wide Tie and Vintage Tee printed papers. *Note: The iris-folding strips are not folded in half for this design.*

2 Adhere strips to reverse side of star cutout, arranging and overlapping pieces as desired.

3 Trim any ends of strips that extend beyond edges of card stock.

Finishing

1 Center and adhere iris-folded panel to card front using dimensional foam tape.

2 Using die cutter and dies, cut a 2 x 1½-inch oval from white card stock and a 2¼ x 1¾-inch oval from black card stock. Stamp "America the Beautiful" onto white oval.

3 Center and adhere white oval to black oval. Adhere oval to card in lower right corner as shown.

4 Punch three stars from white card stock; adhere stars, evenly spaced, down left side of card. ✹

Sources: Printed papers from BasicGrey; stamps from Cornish Heritage Farms; die cutter and dies from Spellbinder Paper Arts; Zip Dry Paper Glue from Beacon Adhesives Inc.

Materials

Card stock: red, white, dark blue, black
Boxer printed papers: Wide Tie, Vintage Tee
Kim Hughes stamps: large Supah Star, "America the Beautiful"
⅞-inch star punch
Corner rounder
Die-cutting machine
Nestabilities small classic oval dies (#S4 112)
Sewing machine with white thread
Dimensional foam tape
Instant-dry paper glue

Through the Window

DESIGN BY **SHARON M. REINHART**

1 Form a 5½ x 5½-inch side-folded card from ivory card stock.

2 Cut a 4½ x 4½-inch piece of Bohemia printed card stock; set aside.

3 Die-cut a 4-inch scalloped frame from ivory card stock.

Iris Folding

1 Center and stamp square iris-folding pattern on a 4¼-inch square of white card stock; this will serve as pattern.

2 Position die-cut frame right side down with pattern centered in opening; adhere with low-tack or removable tape.

3 Cut two 12-inch strips from each of the four ribbons.

4 Referring to photo throughout, plan layout of ribbons. Position ribbon A on reverse side of square in lower right corner, aligning edge of ribbon slightly below line on pattern. *Note: Because you will be using ⅜-inch-wide ribbons on a pattern designed for ½-inch-wide strips, all ribbons should be placed slightly below their respective pattern lines. Adhere one end of ribbon to die-cut frame; trim excess and adhere at opposite end.*

5 In the same manner, adhere ribbon B in upper right corner, ribbon C in upper left corner and ribbon D in lower left corner. Continue until three strips of ribbon have been adhere in each corner.

6 Remove low-tack or removable tape.

Finishing

1 Center and adhere iris-folded panel to Bohemia printed card-stock square using adhesive foam tape.

Materials

Card stock: ivory, white
Bohemia printed card stock
1⅛-inch pink paper flower
Iris-folding square pattern rubber stamp
Black or brown ink pad
Antique copper brad
Dashes, Dots and Checks ⅜-inch-wide complementary printed ribbons: white-on-white, brown with pink stitching, brown/pink dots, brown/pink/blue checks
Die cutter
Sizzix 4-inch scalloped frame die
Piercing tool
Tape: cellophane, double-sided, low-tack or removable
Foam mounting tape
Glue stick

2 Punch hole in center of iris-folded design; attach paper flower with brad.

3 Center and adhere Bohemia printed card stock with iris-folded design to card front as shown. ✳

Sources: Printed card stock from My Mind's Eye; rubber stamp from Stamp N Plus Scrap N; ribbon from Michaels Stores Inc.; Sizzix die cutter and die from Ellison/Sizzix.

Elegant Best Wishes

DESIGN BY **SHARON M. REINHART**

1 Form a 5½ x 4¼-inch top-folded card from white card stock.

2 Cut a 5¼ x 4-inch piece of black/white printed card stock; set aside.

3 Cut a 5 x 3¾-inch piece of black card stock. Center and punch a 1⅞-inch square in card stock ¾ inch from left edge.

Iris Folding

1 Center and stamp square iris-folding pattern on a 4¼-inch square of white card stock; this will serve as pattern.

2 Position black card stock right side down with pattern centered in punched opening; adhere with low-tack or removable tape.

3 Cut two 12 x ½-inch strips each from dark gray shimmery and handmade white floral specialty papers. Cut four 12 x ½-inch strips from black/white printed card stock—two strips from each side of card stock. **Note:** *The iris-folding strips are not folded in half for this design.*

4 Referring to photo throughout, plan position of colors. **Note:** *On sample, strip A is dark gray shimmery, strip B is black/white printed card stock side 1, strip C is handmade white floral paper and strip D is black/white printed card stock side 2.* Position strip A on reverse side of square in lower right corner, aligning edge of strip with line on pattern. Adhere one end of orange strip to lime card stock; trim excess and adhere at opposite end.

5 In the same manner, adhere strip B in upper right corner, strip C in upper left corner and strip D in lower left corner. Continue until all areas are filled except center square.

6 Remove low-tack or removable tape.

FABULOUS FOLDS FOR CARD MAKING

Materials

Card stock: black/white printed, black, white
Specialty papers: dark gray shimmery, handmade white embossed floral
Iris-folding square pattern rubber stamp
Black or brown ink pad
Silver "Best Wishes" stickers
Red heart rhinestone
1⅞-inch square punch
Tape: cellophane, double-sided, low-tack or removable
Foam mounting tape
Glue stick

Finishing

1 Center and adhere iris-folded panel to card front using adhesive foam tape.

2 Cut four 1⅞ x ¼-inch strips of black/white printed card stock; adhere strips beside edges of window leaving 1/16-inch margins.

3 Adhere red rhinestone heart in center of iris-folded design. Adhere stickers to right side of card front as shown. ❋

Sources: Rubber stamp from Stamp N Plus Scrap N; Peel Off stickers from POP-UPs by Plane Class; punch from McGill.

Thank You Berry Much

DESIGN BY **KELLY ANNE GRUNDHAUSER**

Project Note

Adhere elements using instant-dry paper glue unless instructed otherwise.

1 Form a 4½ x 5½-inch top-folded card from card stock with pink side on outside.

2 Punch bottom edge of card front with scallop punch.

3 Using pattern on page 174 and referring to photo throughout, cut strawberry from card front, positioning cutout at an angle 1¼ inches from top.

Iris Folding

1 Cut two or three 1½-inch-wide strips from each of the three pink printed papers, cutting the length of the paper sheet; fold strips in half, wrong sides facing, to form ¾-inch-wide strips.

2 Open card and turn wrong side up. Adhere first strip of color A down right side of strawberry about ½ inch from edge with folded edge toward center. **Note:** *Adhere strip from one end of folded strip; cut and use the same strip to add following strips until it is used up.*

3 In the same manner, adhere the first strip of color B up the left edge of the strawberry; and the first strip of color C across the top.

4 Continue working around the strawberry, adding strips in order, overlapping strips and fanning them out at angles of 15–30 degrees as desired to keep pattern even and consistent.

5 Continue adding strips in order until only a small open opening remains in center. Adhere printed paper of your choice right side down to reverse side of design to cover center.

Materials

Pink/fuchsia double-sided card stock
Printed papers: light green, 3 complementary pinks
"Thank you berry much" stamp
Chalk inks: red, white
⅜-inch-wide pink/fuchsia/white striped ribbon
Pink felt brad
Paper piercer
Scalloped border punch
Double-sided tape
Adhesive foam dots
Instant-dry paper glue

Finishing

1 Close card. Using pattern on page 174, cut strawberry top from green printed paper; adhere over to of strawberry as shown.

2 Stamp sentiment onto lower right corner of card front using white; overstamp sentiment using red and offsetting stamped image slightly.

3 Adhere ribbon to card front near bottom as shown, forming four loops; secure with double-sided tape and adhesive foam dots. Trim right end of ribbon at an angle.

4 Pierce ribbon and card in center of loops; attach brad.

5 Adhere complementary printed paper or card stock to reverse side of card front using double-sided tape. ❋

Sources: Card stock from WorldWin Papers; printed papers from K&Company and Prima Marketing; stamp from Papertrey Ink; chalk ink from Clearsnap Inc.; brad from Queen & Co.; punch from Martha Stewart; Zip Dry Paper Glue from Beacon Adhesives Inc.

Flower Power

DESIGN BY **SHARON M. REINHART**

1 Form a 4¼ x 5½-inch side-folded card from lime card stock.

2 Cut a 4 x 5¼-inch piece of printed paper; center and adhere to card front.

3 Cut a 3¾ x 5-inch piece of lime card stock. Center and punch a 1⅞-inch square in card stock 1³⁄₁₆ inch from top edge.

Iris Folding

1 Center and stamp square iris-folding pattern on a 4¼-inch square of white card stock; this will serve as pattern.

2 Position lime card stock right side down with pattern centered in punched opening; adhere with low-tack or removable tape.

3 Cut two 12 x ½-inch strips each from pink, orange and turquoise card stock and printed paper. **Note:** *The iris-folding strips are not folded in half for this design.*

4 Referring to photo throughout, plan position of colors. **Note:** *On sample, strip A is orange, strip B is turquoise, strip C is printed paper and strip D is pink. Position strip A on reverse side of square in lower right corner, aligning strip edge with pattern line. Adhere one end of orange strip to lime card stock; trim excess and adhere at opposite end.*

5 In the same manner, adhere strip B in upper right corner, strip C in upper left corner and strip D in lower left corner. Continue until all areas are filled except center square.

6 Remove low-tack or removable tape.

Materials
Card stock: white, textured lime, pink, orange and turquoise
Light green floral printed paper
Lightweight cardboard
Iris-folding square pattern rubber stamp
Black ink pad
¼-inch self-adhesive rhinestone flowers: 7 pink, 1 light green
1⅞-inch square punch
Tape: cellophane, double-sided, low-tack or removable
Foam mounting tape
Glue stick

Finishing

1 Center and adhere iris-folded panel to card front using adhesive foam tape.

2 Cut four 1⅞ x ¼-inch strips of printed paper; adhere strips along edges of punched window.

3 Adhere pink rhinestone flowers in corners of printed-paper frame; adhere another pink rhinestone flower in center of iris-folded design.

4 Cut a 2¾ x ½-inch strip of printed paper and adhere to a 2¾ x ½-inch strip of lightweight cardboard. Center and adhere strip to card front 1⅛ inches from bottom edge using adhesive foam tape.

5 Center and adhere remaining rhinestone flowers to printed-paper strip, spacing them evenly and positioning light green flower in center. ❋

Sources: Card stock from Bazzill Basics Paper; printed paper from Doodlebug Design Inc.; rubber stamp from Stamp N Plus Scrap N; punch from McGill.

Happy Anniversary

DESIGN BY **MELANIE DOUTHIT**

1 Form a 5½ x 4¼-inch top-folded card from olive green card stock.

2 Cut a 5½ x 4¼-inch piece of light green card stock; center and cut a 3-inch circle in card stock ¼ inch from top edge. Trim bottom edge with decorative edge scissors; ink all edges.

Iris Folding

1 Cut approximately 18 (2 x 1-inch) strips from printed paper; fold in half, wrong sides facing, to form 2 x ½-inch strips.

2 Referring to photo throughout, adhere folded strips to reverse side of circle around edge, arranging overlapped pieces at an angle so that only folded edges of strips are visible from front. Trim any ends of strips that extend beyond edges of card stock.

Finishing

1 Center and adhere iris-folded panel right side up to card front. Machine-stitch around light green cardstock near edges as shown.

2 Center and adhere chipboard heart to card in opening. Adhere anniversary sticker to olive green card stock; trim, leaving narrow borders. Adhere to card front, overlapping circle as shown.

3 Use die-cutting machine and die cartridge to cut two ¹¹⁄₁₆-inch photo corners from olive green card stock and two ⅞-inch photo corners from printed paper. Center and adhere card-stock photo corners to printed paper photo corners; adhere to card in top corners.

4 Use die-cutting machine and die to die-cut butterfly from printed paper; adhere to right edge of card as shown.

5 Adhere rickrack across bottom edge of card; adhere buttons on left side as shown. ✸

Sources: Printed paper from BasicGrey; card-stock sticker from Melissa Frances; chipboard from Making Memories; decorative-edge scissors from Fiskars; Cuttlebug die-cutting machine and die (butterfly) and Cricut die-cutting machine and die cartridge (photo corners) from Provo Craft; Zip Dry Paper Glue from Beacon Adhesives Inc.

Materials
Card stock: light green, olive green
Charming printed paper
"Happy Anniversary" card-stock sticker
Garden Party chipboard heart
Assorted small pink buttons
Light brown ink
Pink jumbo rickrack
Die-cutting machines
2 x 6-inch Nature & Texture Blocks die #37-1117
Celebrations die cartridge #29-0020
Decorative-edge scissors
Sewing machine with white thread
Instant-dry paper glue

Bloomin' Vase

DESIGN BY **LISA SILVER**

Project Note

Adhere elements using paper adhesive unless instructed otherwise.

1 Form a 4¼ x 5½-inch top-folded card from light pink card stock.

2 Cut a 4¼ x 5½-inch piece of spring green card stock; adhere to card front.

Iris Folding

1 Cut a 4 x 5¼-inch piece of Swell printed paper. Stamp vase on printed paper 1⅛ inches from right edge and ⅝ inch from bottom edge; stamp flower stems in top of vase; color leaves with markers.

2 Cut out vase just inside stamped outline; lay printed paper right side down.

3 Cut about eight 1½ x 1-inch strips each from the Citron, Peony and Fandango printed papers.
Note: *The iris-folding strips are not folded in half for this design.*

4 Referring to photo throughout, adhere strips to reverse side of vase cutout, arranging and overlapping pieces as desired. Entire opening should be covered.

5 Trim any ends of strips that extend beyond edges of card stock. Secure strips as needed with adhesive tape.

Finishing

1 Cut a 1¼ x 5¼-inch strip of deep pink card stock; adhere to right side of vase panel with left, top and bottom edges even.

2 Cut a 1 x 5¼-inch strip of Fashionable printed paper; remove guide from corner rounder and punch scallops along right edge. Center and pierce a hole in each scallop; highlight holes with white gel pen. Adhere strip to vase panel with left, top and bottom edges even.

3 Stamp one bloom each on Peony, Fandango and Citron printed papers; cut out. Embellish blooms as desired with markers and glitter pens.

4 Adhere blooms to stems on vase panel as shown, adhering center bloom with adhesive foam tape for dimension.

5 Stamp "hugs" on vase panel near lower left corner.

6 Center and adhere vase panel to card front using adhesive foam tape. ✸

Sources: Printed papers from BasicGrey; stamp sets from Cornish Heritage Farms; Copic markers; Spica glitter pens; corner rounder from EK Success Ltd.

Materials
Card stock: spring green, deep pink, light pink
Sultry printed papers: Swell, Fashionable, Fandango, Citron, Peony
Kim Hughes stamp sets: Bloomin' Beautiful, Vases, Scripty Words
Black dye ink
Markers
Glitter pens
White gel pen
Corner rounder
Piercing tool
Foam mounting tape
Adhesive tape
Paper adhesive

Thank You Tree

DESIGN BY **LISA SILVER**

Project Note

Adhere elements using instant-dry paper glue unless instructed otherwise.

1 Form a 4¼ x 5½-inch top-folded card from orange card stock; ink edges orange.

2 Cut a 4 x 5¼-inch piece of Equinox printed paper; ink edges sepia.

Iris Folding

1 Referring to photo throughout, stamp black tree onto Seasoned printed paper. Trim out the tree trunk; discard the rest of the image.

2 Stamp the same tree in black onto the rectangle of Equinox printed paper cut earlier, positioning treetop 1 inch from top edge and ¾ inch from right edge.

3 Partially ink grid backgrounder stamp with black ink; stamp onto printed paper over top portion of tree.

4 Carefully trim out inside of treetop.

5 Cut 1-inch-wide strips of light green, medium green and medium brown card stock. **Note:** *The iris-folding strips are not folded in half for this design.*

6 Referring to photo throughout, adhere strips to reverse side of tree cutout, arranging and overlapping pieces as desired. Add just a few brown strips to give the appearance of tree branches.

7 Trim any ends of strips that extend beyond edges of card stock.

Materials

Card stock: light green, medium green, medium brown, white, orange
Mellow printed papers: Seasoned, Equinox, Slack
Kim Hughes Making the Grade stamp set
Grid paper backgrounder stamp
Inks: black dye, orange and sepia distress
White pigment pen
Small complementary buttons
10 inches ¼-inch-wide brown grosgrain ribbon
Paper punches: ⅛-inch hole, 1-inch circle punch
Die cutter
2½ x ⅝-inch ribbon tag die
Foam mounting tape
Instant-dry paper glue

Finishing

1 Adhere brown tree trunk to Equinox printed paper over stamped image.

2 Cut a ¾ x 5¼-inch strip of Slack printed paper with stripes running horizontally; adhere to iris-folded panel ¼ inch from left edge. Center and adhere panel to card front using adhesive foam tape around edges.

3 Die-cut tag from white card stock. Stamp sentiment on tag in black; ink edges sepia. Thread ribbon through tag and wrap around card front 1½ inches from bottom edge, adhering ends on reverse side.

4 Adhere buttons to card front as shown. Add faux stitches to holes using white pigment pen. ✺

Sources: Printed papers from BasicGrey; stamp set and backgrounder stamp from Cornish Heritage Farms; inks and pigment pen from Ranger Industries; Nestabilities ribbon tag die from Spellbinder Paper Arts; Zip Dry Paper Glue from Beacon Adhesives Inc.

Autumn Tree

DESIGN BY **KELLY ANNE GRUNDHAUSER**

Project Note

Adhere elements using instant-dry paper glue unless instructed otherwise.

1 Form a 5 x 6-inch top-folded card from Sandcastle printed card stock.

2 Using pattern on page 174 and referring to photo throughout, cut circle for treetop from card front, positioning cutout ½ inch from left edge and ⅝ inch from top fold. Reserve circle to use later.

Iris Folding

1 Cut two or three 1½-inch-wide strips from each of the four printed papers, cutting the length of the paper sheet; fold strips in half, wrong sides facing, to create ¾-inch-wide strips.

2 Open card and turn wrong side up. Adhere first strip of color A across bottom of circle about ½ inch from edge with folded edge toward center. **Note:** *Adhere strip from one end of folded strip; cut and use the same strip to add following strips until it is used up.*

3 In the same manner, adhere the first strip of color B up the left edge of the circle; the first strip of color C across the top; and the first strip of color D down the right edge.

4 Continue working around the circle, adding strips in order, overlapping strips and fanning them out at angles of 15–30 degrees as desired to keep pattern even and consistent.

5 Continue adding strips in order until only a small open square—about ½ inch—remains in center. Adhere reserved circle of Sandcastle printed card stock right side down to reverse side of design to cover center.

Materials

Printed card stock: Brownie, Sandcastle, cream, orange
4 complementary printed papers
"Autumn" stamp
Brown chalk ink
Natural raffia
Decorative fiber
Scallop punch
Double-sided tape
Instant-dry paper glue

6 If desired, adhere complementary printed paper or card stock to reverse side of card front using double-sided tape.

Finishing

1 Close card. Cut a 5 x 1-inch strip of cream card stock and a 5 x ½-inch strip of orange card stock. Punch right end of cream strip with scallop punch; ink edges.

2 Adhere cream card-stock strip to card front ½ inch from bottom; adhere orange strip to card front just below cream card-stock strip.

3 Stamp sentiment on cream card-stock strip to right of tree.

4 Tie raffia and decorative fiber around card front above card-stock strips. Adhere ends of fiber on reverse side. Tie raffia ends in a multiloop bow on front to left of tree.

5 Using pattern on page 174, cut tree trunk from Brownie printed card stock; adhere to card as shown. ✳

Sources: All in the Family printed card stock from Core'dinations; printed papers from SEI; Kim Hughes stamp from Cornish Heritage Farms; decorative fiber from Making Memories; Zip Dry Paper Glue from Beacon Adhesives Inc.

ACCORDION
FOLDS

Accordion fold cards are among the most versatile of folding techniques. The construction of the mountains and valleys on these cards is limited only by your imagination. Create tight folds for a flip-flop card design or use a wider fold design for an attractive tri-fold greeting card.

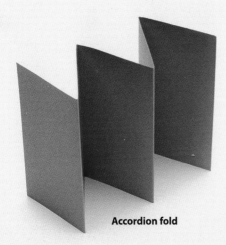

Accordion fold

Like the musical instrument for which they are named, accordion cards are pleated—back-and-forth folds that create dimension and excitement. Picture a mountain range with valleys between the peaks. Accordion cards use terminology borrowed from the landscape. Folds that extend upward are called "mountain" folds, while those that dip down are "valley" folds.

Diagrams for accordion cards use two different kinds of dotted lines for the two kinds of folds, or two different colors—and it is important to get the mountain and valley folds in the right places.

With a simple card that is folded in half, the scoring and folding is important but not critical. You can always trim a bit if you're off-center. With accordion cards, however, take your time—careful measuring, scoring and folding spell the difference between a terrific accordion card and a lopsided disaster.

Proportion is a key element in accordion cards. If folds are close together, the effect is akin to a fan. The smaller the card, the closer the folds can be. For example, folds that are spaced at 1-inch intervals work fine for a gift tag, but panels on a traditional card are usually 2 to 4 inches wide.

Folds can be evenly or unevenly spaced, and accordion cards can fold from a center panel, forming pleated panels both left and right and/or heading in one direction (left to right) only.

All of the elements on an accordion card can be contained within the panels; or they can extend beyond the folds, peeking out when the card is closed, but often revealing more when the card is opened.

Getting Started

Because accordion cards often require long strips of card stock, you may need to glue pieces together. Measure and cut the strip to the dimensions required.

Z-fold

If you have a scoring board, use the ruler across the top to measure and position each score line. Flip the card stock, alternating right side up and right side down, as you score lines for mountain and valley folds.

For other scoring tools, measure carefully, and make light pencil marks for guidelines. A quilting ruler with a grid is helpful.

More Possibilities

By making additional cuts and folds to alter the shape and direction of the panels, you can give your accordion cards an entirely different look—a look with more complexity and dimension, but only a little bit more work. Turn accordion cards into flip-flop cards or Z-fold cards with these simple changes and additions. ✳

Flip-flop card

Top Secret

DESIGN BY **LINDA BEESON**

1 *Accordion-fold spine:* Cut a piece of Loveland Ruby Avenue printed paper 4 x 4¼ inches. Score printed paper vertically ¾ inch, 1¼ inches, 1¾ inches, 2¼ inches, 2¾ inches and 3¼ inches from left edge. Fold paper accordion-style; pin-dot side will be inside card and large red dots will be on outside.

2 *Front and back:* Cut two pieces 5½ x 4½ inches from Loveland Jade Drive printed paper. Green-on-green dot side will be on outside.

3 Using corner rounder punch, round off corners of card front, back and spine.

4 Referring to photo throughout, embellish card front with Kewel Frames stamped in green and the smaller image from Kewel Frame stamp set stamped in black. Stamp "Top Secret" from Art Espionage 4 stamp set onto card front using black.

5 Adhere front flap of spine to left edge of card front; adhere back flap of spine to card's back cover. Folds of spine will be inside card.

6 Cut a 7 x 1¼-inch strip of Loveland Ruby Avenue paper; using corner rounder punch, round off corners on one end. Center and adhere

Materials

Printed paper: Loveland Jade Drive, White Line Background, Loveland Ruby Avenue
Stamp sets: Art Espionage 4, Kewel Frame, Pay Your Dues-Greetings
Ink pads: black, green, magenta
Clear rhinestone
3 deep pink brads
Corner rounder
Paper folder
Paper adhesive

strip horizontally across back of card; wrap rounded end around spine and adhere to card front. Stamp black flourish on end of strip; adhere rhinestone to stamped motif.

7 Cut three strips of White Line Background paper 4½ x 1¼ inches; round off ends on right edge of each using corner rounder punch. Ink edges green. Align strips horizontally edge to edge; stamp green Kewel Frame over all three strips.

8 Using black ink, stamp "Happy" onto one strip, "Birthday" onto the next and "To You" onto the bottom strip. Using magenta ink, stamp flourishes on ends of strips as shown.

9 Use brads to attach a strip to each fold of spine inside card. ✳

Sources: Printed paper from Scenic Route Paper Co.; stamps from Art Declassified; brads from Creative Impressions; Scor-Pal Products paper folder.

Best Wishes

DESIGN BY **LINDSEY BOTKIN**

1 Cut a piece of brown card stock 11¼ x 4¼ inches. Score card stock vertically 2½ and 5 inches from left edge. Fold card in half, then fold narrower panel back to left.

2 Cut a 2¼ x 4-inch piece of orange pin-dot printed paper; referring to photo throughout, center and adhere to front panel.

3 Cut a 2¼ x 4-inch piece of orange/green printed paper; center and adhere to narrow panel inside card.

4 Piece together assorted colors and widths of printed paper to make a panel 6 x 4 inches; center and adhere to large panel inside card.

Sparrows

1 Stamp two sparrows onto white card stock; color with markers.

2 *Card front:* Trim a 2¼ x 2⅛-inch rectangle around one sparrow; adhere to brown card stock and trim, leaving ⅛-inch borders.

3 Pierce three pairs of holes for faux "stitching" over edge of sparrow panel near lower left corner and upper right corner; connect pairs of holes with "stitches" using brown marker.

Materials

Card stock: brown, white
Lucid printed papers: pale yellow, orange/green print, orange/yellow pin-dot
Beige paper hydrangea petals: 2-inch, 2 (1⅜-inch)
Stamps: sparrow, Best Wishes
Brown solvent-based ink
Markers
2 silver mini brads
2 magnetic card closures
12 inches ⅜-inch-wide pale cream satin ribbon
Paper piercer
Paper adhesive

4 Center and adhere a small blossom to large blossom using a mini brad; adhere to lower right corner of sparrow panel. Adhere half of a magnetic closure to reverse side of blossoms.

5 Adhere sparrow panel to card front 1¼ inches from left edge and ⅝ inch from top edge.

6 *Inside card:* Trim second sparrow panel to 2⅛ x 2 inches; adhere inside card 1½ inches from fold and ⅞ inch from top edge. Pierce faux stitching holes along left edge; connect with stitches using brown marker. Add stitches along edges of printed paper strips as desired.

7 Pierce remaining blossom with mini brad; adhere inside card so that it will align with magnetic closure.

Finishing

1 Stamp "Best Wishes" onto lower right corner of card.

2 Wrap ribbon around front panel ⅝ inch from left edge; knot near top and trim ends.

3 Close card; adhere remaining magnetic closure between narrow flaps near left edge to hold card closed. ✱

Sources: Printed papers and hydrangea blossoms from Prima Marketing; stamps from Inkadinkado; solvent-based ink from Tsukineko Inc.; Copic markers; blender pen from Stampin' Up; magnetic card closures from BasicGrey.

Celebrate

DESIGN BY **LINDSEY BOTKIN**

Project Note

Adhere elements using paper adhesive unless instructed otherwise.

1 Cut a 5½ x 6⅜-inch piece of pink card stock. Score card stock horizontally 2⅛ inches from top edge; fold top panel down to front.

2 *Back panel:* Cut a 5¼ x 4-inch piece of white card stock for back panel. Referring to photo throughout, stamp butterflies and "Celebrate!" onto white card stock using black ink. Color butterflies with pink and green inks using blender pen; center and adhere to back panel.

3 *Top panel:* Cut a 5 x 2-inch piece of white card stock; center and adhere to top panel. Cut a

Materials

Card stock: pink, white
Green Garden Party printed paper
Clear stamp sets: Cupcakes, Patterned Bugs
Ink: black solvent-based, pink, light green
Blender pen
White gel pen
Frosted white glitter glue
⅝-inch-wide white brad
⁷⁄₁₆-inch-wide sheer white pin-dot ribbon
Magnetic card closure
Paper-piercing tool
Punches: 2-inch circle, 2½-inch scalloped circle
Adhesive foam dots
Paper adhesive

5 x 1-inch piece of Green Garden Party printed paper; adhere to white card stock ¼ inch from bottom edge.

4 Pierce holes across top of printed paper strip ⅛ inch from edge; using white gel pen, connect holes to with faux "stitches."

5 Wrap ribbon around top panel; knot ends on front near right edge. Adhere halves of magnetic closure to reverse side of top panel and front back panel.

6 *Scalloped medallion:* Punch 2½-inch scalloped circle from pink card stock. Stamp black butterfly onto white card stock; punch 2-inch circle around stamped image. Center and adhere stamped circle to pink scalloped circle. Stamp pink butterfly onto white card stock; cut out and embellish with glitter glue. Adhere pink butterfly to black butterfly using adhesive foam dot. Center medallion on card as shown; adhere to top flap.

7 Pierce hole through back panel of card and attach white brad so that it catches edge of top flap. ✸

Sources: Printed paper from Making Memories; stamp sets from Inkadinkado; solvent-based ink from Tsukineko Inc.; blender pen from Stampin' Up!; Stickles glitter glue from Ranger Industries; brad from American Crafts; punches from Uchida of America.

Make a Wish

DESIGN BY **MELANIE DOUTHIT**

Materials
Card stock: dark blue, brown
Printed papers: Foyer Floral, Foyer
   Flourish, blue
Birthday stamp #50432
Blue ink
Die-cutting machine
Celebrations die cartridge #29-0020
4½ inches white decorative trim
Instant-dry paper glue

1 Cut an 11 x 4¼-inch piece of dark blue card stock. Score card stock vertically 5½ inches from left edge; close card, then score front flap 2¾ inches from fold and fold it to the left to form a Z-fold card.

2 Referring to photo throughout, cut a piece of Foyer Floral printed paper 2⅝ x 4⅛ inches; ink edges blue. Center and adhere printed paper to front (left) flap. Adhere decorative trim down left edge.

3 Cut a piece of blue printed paper 5⅜ x 4⅛ inches; ink edges. Center and adhere blue paper to larger inner panel.

4 Use die-cutting machine and die cartridge to cut a small cupcake cup and ¾-inch photo corner from Foyer Flourish printed paper; cut complete cupcake, four ½-inch photo corners and one 1⅛-inch photo corner from brown card stock.

5 Cut a 2-inch square of blue printed paper; ink edges blue. Center and adhere printed paper to dark blue card stock; trim, leaving narrow borders.

6 Center and adhere cupcake and cupcake cup to blue square; adhere brown photo corners to corners of square as shown. Center square on card ⅜ inch from top; adhere square to front flap.

7 Center and adhere Foyer Flourish photo corner to large brown photo corner; adhere to upper right corner of card as shown.

8 Using blue ink, stamp "Make a Wish!" onto lower right corner card. ✺

Sources: Foyer printed papers from Chatterbox; See D's stamp from Darice Inc.; Cricut die-cutting machine and cartridge from Provo Craft; Zip Dry Paper Glue from Beacon Adhesives Inc.

Serenity

DESIGN BY KERI LEE SEREIKA

1 Cut an 11 x 4¼-inch piece of light green card stock. Score card stock vertically 2¾ and 5½ inches from left edge. Fold card accordion-style.

2 Referring to photo throughout, stamp front left panel repeatedly with vintage blossom using spring green ink. Stamp floral swirls along right edge of card using spring green ink; overstamp swirls with charcoal swirls for shadow effect.

3 Pierce hole in card 1⅛ inches from top edge and 1 inch from right edge; attach flower with brad.

Stamped Tag

1 Cut a 3¼ x 2¼-inch piece of Crème Brulee card stock; center and stamp sentiment onto card stock using charcoal ink.

2 Adhere stamped tag to dark red card stock and trim, leaving narrow borders. Adhere to red card stock and trim, leaving narrow borders.

3 Adhere stamped tag to left front panel only, ⅞ inch from left edge and ⅜ inch from

bottom edge. **Option:** *Cut a small diagonal slit in right panel of card under flower petals; tuck upper right corner of stamped tag into slit to hold card closed.*

Materials

Card stock: red, dark red, light green, Crème Brulee metallic
Serenity stamp set
Ink pads: dark gray chalk, spring green dye
1¾-inch brown shimmery flower with leaves
⁵⁄₁₆-inch light brown shimmery brad
12 inches ¼-inch-wide brown grosgrain ribbon
Paper piercer
Paper adhesive

Finishing

Wrap ribbon around front left panel of card ½ inch from left edge. Knot ribbon ends on front near bottom; trim as desired. ✱

Sources: Metallic card stock from Prism Papers; stamp set from Artistic Outpost; chalk ink from Clearsnap Inc.; flower and brad from Creative Impressions.

You're Out of This World

DESIGN BY **LINDSEY BOTKIN**

Materials
Card stock: off-white, brown, orange
Printed papers: Ebb, Harvested
Out of This World stamp set
Black ink pad
Markers
5¼ inches pumpkin-colored rickrack
Magnetic card closure
Dimensional adhesive foam dot
Paper adhesive

Project Note

Adhere elements using paper adhesive unless instructed otherwise.

1 Cut an 8½ x 5½-inch piece of off-white card stock. Score card stock vertically 2⅛ and 4¼ inches from left edge.

2 Cut two pieces of Harvested printed paper 1⅞ x 5¼ inches; center and adhere printed paper to two narrower panels. Cut a piece of Ebb printed paper 4¼ x 5¼ inches; center and adhere to larger panel at right.

3 Stamp astronaut on off-white card stock. Referring to photo throughout, color image with markers. Trim 1⅞ x 2¼-inch rectangle around stamped image and adhere to brown card stock; cut out, leaving ⅛-inch borders. Center image on closed card 1¼ inches from top; adhere to left panel. Adhere rickrack to left panel near left edge as shown.

4 Adhere magnetic card closure between narrow panels near left edge to help close card.

5 Stamp, color and cut out moon and rocket; adhere as shown near bottom edge of a 3 x 3¾-inch piece of off-white card stock. Adhere card stock inside card ⅞ inch from top and ¼ inch from left fold.

6 Stamp "You're out of this world!" on off-white card stock; trim small rectangle around words and adhere to orange card stock. Cut out, leaving narrow borders. Adhere to lower right corner of card.

7 Stamp, color and cut out Saturn. With card closed, adhere Saturn to card with a dimensional adhesive foam dot so that Saturn just overlaps upper right corner of astronaut panel. ✴

Sources: Mellow printed papers and magnetic card closure from BasicGrey; stamp set from Lizzie Anne Designs; Copic markers; rickrack from Daisy D's Paper Co.

Best Buddies

DESIGN BY **KELLY ANNE GRUNDHAUSER**

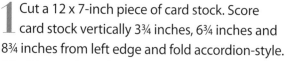

1 Cut a 12 x 7-inch piece of card stock. Score card stock vertically 3¾ inches, 6¾ inches and 8¾ inches from left edge and fold accordion-style.

2 Distress far right edge of card; ink distressed edge.

3 Cut a 3 x 5-inch piece of striped printed paper; trim one short edge with scallop punch. Distress straight edges; ink all edges brown. Referring to photo throughout, adhere printed paper to card front, scalloped edge at the top, ½ inch from top and ¼ inch from left edge.

4 Distress edges of card-stock sticker; ink edges green. Adhere to card over printed paper, 1⅛ inches from top and ⅜ inch from left edge.

5 Lightly ink rickrack with brown ink; adhere along right edge of card front.

6 Lightly ink felt brad with brown and green inks. Pierce hole in card front 2 inches from bottom and ⅝ inch from right edge. Stamp floral motif onto tiny tag using brown ink. If tag has no hanger, thread onto brown thread; wrap thread around prongs of felt brad and attach brad in hole.

Materials

Burnt orange card stock
Brothers Stripe printed paper
Brothers Wild Descriptives card-stock sticker
Tiny white card-stock tag
Stamps: tiny floral, "youth is a circumstance" sentiment
Ink: dark brown, green
White felt brad
Brown thread (optional)
7 inches green velvet rickrack
Simple Scallop Edge Punch
Edge distresser
Paper piercer
Instant-dry paper glue

7 *Inside card:* Cut a 3 x 4-inch piece of striped printed paper; punch one short edge with scallop punch. Distress straight edges; ink all edges brown. With scalloped edge at top, stamp sentiment onto printed paper using brown ink. Adhere inside card on second panel, 1¼ inches from top and ⅜ inch from fold. ❋

Sources: Printed paper and card-stock sticker from My Mind's Eye; stamps from Cloud 9; felt brad from Queen & Co.; punch from Martha Stewart; edge distresser from Tonic Studios; Zip Dry Paper Glue from Beacon Adhesives Inc.

Modern Lily

DESIGN BY **KERI LEE SEREIKA**

Materials

Card stock: dark spring green, light spring green, salmon pink, Crème Brulee metallic
Pink Lemonade printed papers: Lulubelle, Sweetpea
Modern Lily stamp
Chalk ink pads: pink, mossy green
3 inches light green baby rickrack
12 inches ½-inch-wide pink swirls sheer organdy ribbon
4 green mini brads
Copper spiral paper clip
Paper piercer
Paper adhesive
Adhesive foam tape

Project Note
Adhere elements using paper adhesive unless instructed otherwise.

Salmon Pink Card

1 Cut an 8½ x 4¼-inch piece of salmon pink card stock. Score card stock vertically 3½ inches from left edge.

2 Cut a 3¼ x 4-inch piece of Sweetpea printed paper; center and adhere to front panel of card.

3 Referring to photo throughout, wrap ribbon around front panel near fold. Knot ends on front near top; trim as desired.

Dark Spring Green Card

1 Cut an 8½ x 3-inch piece of dark spring green card stock. Score card stock vertically 4¼ inches from left edge. Fold card and position with fold along right edge.

2 Cut a 4⅛ x 2⅞-inch piece of Lulubelle printed paper; center and adhere to front panel of card.

3 Adhere rickrack vertically to card 1 inch from fold; fasten copper swirl clip over top edge.

Stamped Panel

1 Ink blossom portion of stamp with pink ink and stem and leaves with mossy green. Without re-inking stamp, stamp three images onto a 2¼-inch square of Crème Brulee card stock.

2 Distress edges of stamped card stock using the edge of a scissors blade.

3 Center and adhere stamped card stock to a 2½-inch square of light spring green card stock; ink edges mossy green.

4 Pierce holes in corners of light spring green card stock; attach mini brads.

Finishing

1 Adhere stamped panel to front of dark spring green card ¼ inch from top and bottom edges and ⅜ inch from left (open) edge using adhesive foam tape.

2 Referring to Fig. 1, page 172, adhere back panel of dark spring green card inside salmon pink card so that green card's fold is aligned with right edge of pink card. Close salmon pink card; close dark spring green card over salmon pink card. ✸

Sources: Metallic card stock from Prism Papers; printed papers from Webster's Pages; stamp from Cornish Heritage Farms; chalk ink from Clearsnap Inc.; ribbon and copper swirl clip from Creative Impressions.

Beauty

DESIGN BY **ROBIN ARNOLD**

1 Cut an 8¼ x 4¼-inch piece of polka-dot/yellow card stock. Score card stock vertically 2¾ inches from left edge. Fold card with solid yellow side facing out.

2 Form a 2¾ x 4½-inch top-folded card from floral/brown card stock with floral side facing out. Referring to photo throughout, adhere back of top-folded card to larger panel of side folded card with right and bottom edges even.

3 Center and adhere a 2½ x 4-inch piece of pink mesh to yellow panel on card front.

4 Using dies and die cutter, cut scalloped rectangles from card stock as follows: 3 x 2⅜-inch from brown card stock; 2¼ x 15/16-inch from polka-dot card stock; 19/16 x 1¼-inch from yellow card stock.

5 Center and stamp "Beauty" on yellow rectangle; center and adhere yellow rectangle to polka-dot rectangle, then to brown rectangle. Center rectangles on closed card; adhere to yellow/mesh flap only.

6 *Inside card:* Stamp "The future belongs …" sentiment onto polka-dot surface.

7 Attach contrasting mini brads to silk flowers, bending prongs flat. Adhere pink flower to card at upper left corner of rectangles and yellow flower at lower right corner of rectangles. ✱

Sources: Card stock from Crate Paper; stamps from Close To My Heart; mesh from Magic Mesh; Wizard die cutter and Nestabilities dies from Spellbinder Paper Arts.

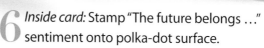

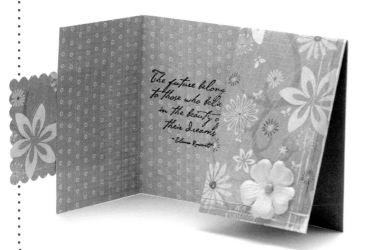

Materials
Twirl collection double-sided card
   stock: pink floral/brown solid, green-
   and-pink polka dots/yellow solid
Stamps: "Beauty," "The future belongs …"
Black ink pad
Pink fine-weave repositionable mesh
1¼-inch silk flowers: pink, yellow
Mini brads: pink, yellow
Die cutter
Classic Scalloped Rectangle dies
   (#S4 133)
Paper adhesive

Thank You

DESIGN BY **LINDSEY BOTKIN**

FABULOUS FOLDS FOR CARD MAKING

1 Cut a piece of striped printed paper 11 x 4¼ inches. Score printed paper vertically 2¾ and 5½ inches from left edge. Fold card in half, then fold narrower panel to left.

2 Cut a 2½ x 4-inch piece of pin-dot printed paper; referring to photo throughout, center and adhere to front panel on left. Cut a ⅜ x 4-inch strip of white card stock; adhere vertically to pin-dot paper ¼ inch from left edge of card. Pierce three evenly spaced holes down center of white strip; attach mini brads.

3 Open card. Cut a 5¼ x 4-inch piece of white card stock; center and adhere to larger panel. Cut a 5¼ x 1¾-inch strip of striped printed paper and a 5¼ x 1⅛-inch strip of pin-dot printed paper. Center and adhere pin-dot strip to striped strip; adhere strips to white card stock 1⅛ inches from top edge of card.

4 Stamp "Thank you" in black onto lower right corner of card. Pierce a hole through center of pin-dot strip 1¼ inches from right edge; attach decorative brad.

5 Stamp poppies in black onto white card stock. Tint image with light blue and pale green inks; blend with blender pen. Trim a 2⅜ x 3⅛-inch rectangle around stamped image; adhere to light green card stock and cut out, leaving narrow borders. Close card; adhere stamped image to front panel ⅞ inch from left edge and ¼ inch from top edge. ✳

Sources: Printed papers from My Mind's Eye; stamps from Inkadinkado; solvent-based ink from Tsukineko Inc.; blender pen from Stampin' Up; decorative brad from Making Memories.

Materials

Card stock: white, light green
Printed papers: beige/cream pin-dot, beige/white/blue stripe
Stamps: poppies, "Thank You"
Ink pads: black solvent-based, light blue, pale green
Blender pen
Brads: 3 pewter mini, ½-inch decorative pewter
Paper piercer
Paper adhesive

Size 6

DESIGN BY **TAMI MAYBERRY**

1 Cut a 7 x 6¼-inch piece of orange card stock. Cut a 6¾ x 6-inch piece of printed paper; center and adhere to card stock. Using zigzag stitch, machine-stitch around edge of printed paper.

2 Referring to Fig. 1, page 171, throughout, score 1-inch vertical lines beginning at top, 3 inches and 4 inches from left edge; repeat at bottom.

3 Cut two 2¾ x 4¼-inch rectangles from orange card stock. Adhere one to center of card between score lines; cut around left and right edges, stopping at scored lines. Flip card over; adhere second rectangle to other side.

4 Fold card along scored lines so that left side is on top.

5 Stamp bathing beauty and Edna images onto white card stock; color with markers and cut out. Adhere images to bright green card stock and trim, leaving narrow borders. Adhere stamped images to center panel so bathing beauty is visible when card is closed.

6 Stamp greeting onto scraps of orange card stock; trim around words and adhere to card as shown.

7 Adhere three rhinestones to card front in a vertical row near lower left corner; adhere remaining rhinestones in a vertical row just outside upper right corner of center cutout.

8 Thread ribbon through opening and wrap around right side of card; slight to bottom of opening and tie ends in a bow. ❋

Sources: Printed paper from My Mind's Eye; stamps from Rubbernecker; Copic markers from Copic.

Materials

Card stock: orange, bright green, white
Bright orange/multicolored plaid printed paper
Stamps: Edna in Swimsuit, Bathing Beauty with Dots, Decorate Text
Black ink pad
Markers
3 tiny orange rhinestones
12 inches ⁷⁄₁₆-inch-wide orange/white pin-dot grosgrain ribbon
Sewing machine with white thread
Paper adhesive

Thank You Bouquet

DESIGN BY **LINDSEY BOTKIN**

Project Note

Adhere elements using paper adhesive unless instructed otherwise.

1 Cut a 6¾ x 5½-inch piece of white card stock.

2 Referring to Fig. 1, page 171, throughout, score 1¼-inch vertical lines beginning at top edge, 2¾ inches and 4 inches from left edge; repeat at bottom edge.

3 Cutting out from scored lines on each side, cut a 3¾ x 3-inch flip-flop panel in center of card, leaving it attached at top and bottom between scored lines.

Flip-flop Panel

1 Cut two 3½ x 2¾-inch rectangles from pink card stock; center and adhere one to each side of flip-flop panel.

2 Stamp Lovely Flowers onto white card stock using brown ink. Tint blossoms and leaves with light green and pink inks; trim around image and adhere to front of flip-flop panel so that it is centered on visible portion of panel when card is closed.

3 Cut a 2¾ x 2½-inch piece of white card stock; stamp pink Blossom onto upper left corner. Over-stamp Thank You across bottom using brown ink; center and adhere to back of flip-flop panel.

Card Front & Back

1 Cut a 2½ x 5 ¼-inch piece of pin-dot printed paper and a 2½ x 5 ¼-inch piece of printed card stock.

2 For front panel, from pin-dot printed paper, cut a 1¼ x 3⅛-inch piece from center of right edge; center and adhere to front (left) panel. For back panel, from printed card stock, cut a 1¼ x 3⅛-inch piece from center of left edge; center and adhere to back (right) panel.

3 Cut a 1⅛ x 1¼-inch piece of Lulubelle printed card stock and a matching piece of printed paper. For front, adhere card stock over printed paper 1¾ inches from top edge of card. For back, adhere printed paper to printed card stock in matching position.

4 Cut ribbon in half; tie one piece around each half of card, over contrasting embellishments added in step 3. Knot on front; trim ribbon ends.

Materials

Lulubelle printed card stock
Solid card stock: pink, white
Beige/white pin-dot printed paper
Stamps: Lovely Flowers, Blossom, "Thank You"
Ink pads: brown solvent-based, pink, light green, white
White flourish rub-on transfer
3 silver mini brads
12 inches ¼-inch-wide white pin-dot sheer ribbon
Adhesive foam dot
Paper adhesive

Finishing

1 Punch three holes across top of front panel as shown; attach mini brads. Apply white flourish rub-on transfer to lower left corner.

2 Stamp Blossom onto white card stock using pink ink. Cut out and adhere to lower right corner on back panel using adhesive foam dot. ✱

Sources: Printed card stock from Webster's Pages; printed paper from Making Memories; stamps from Inkadinkado; solvent-based ink from Tsukineko Inc.; rub-on transfer from me & my BIG ideas.

Birthday Wishes

DESIGN BY **LISA SILVER**

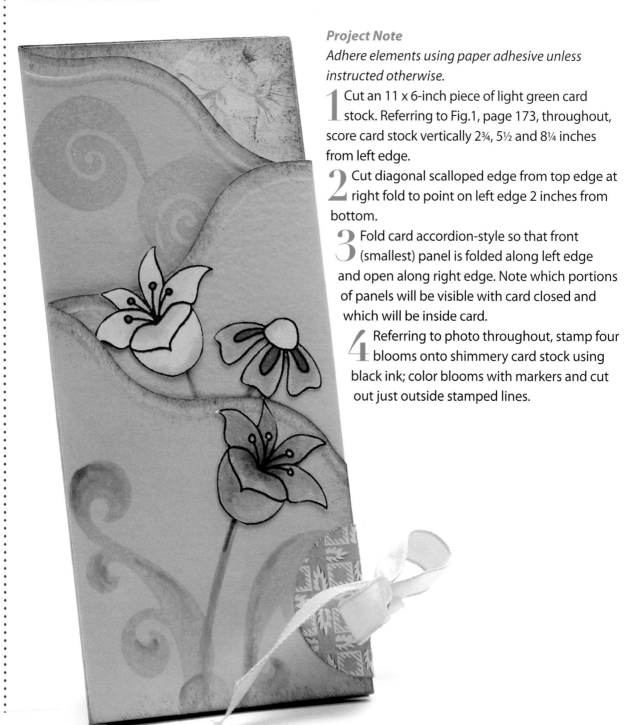

Project Note

Adhere elements using paper adhesive unless instructed otherwise.

1. Cut an 11 x 6-inch piece of light green card stock. Referring to Fig.1, page 173, throughout, score card stock vertically 2¾, 5½ and 8¼ inches from left edge.

2. Cut diagonal scalloped edge from top edge at right fold to point on left edge 2 inches from bottom.

3. Fold card accordion-style so that front (smallest) panel is folded along left edge and open along right edge. Note which portions of panels will be visible with card closed and which will be inside card.

4. Referring to photo throughout, stamp four blooms onto shimmery card stock using black ink; color blooms with markers and cut out just outside stamped lines.

5 Plan placement of flowers on card. For leaves, stamp swirls from Bold Curls stamp set onto card using light green dye ink. Using watercolor brush dipped in water, pick up distress ink and add flower stems and highlights to swirls. Ink edges of card with distress ink.

6 Cut a 2¾ x 6-inch piece of Vogue printed paper; ink edges with distress ink. Stamp "Birthday wishes" (from Silhouette Blooms II stamp set) onto printed paper slightly above center. Adhere printed paper to right panel.

7 Adhere flower blooms to card.

8 *Ribbon closure:* Punch two 1⅜-inch circles from Smart printed paper. Fold circles in half; cut a ½-inch slit in center of each on fold. Cut ribbon in half; thread ½ inch of one end through slit in each circle. Adhere circles and ribbon ends over open edges of front and back panels near bottom. Tie ribbons in a bow; trim ends as desired.

9 Using jewel glue, adhere halves of magnetic closure to wrong side of two center panels where indicated by Xs on Fig. 1, page 173. ✱

Sources: Shimmery card stock from www.CutCardStock.com; printed papers from BasicGrey; stamp sets from Cornish Heritage Farms; Copic markers from Copic; circle punch from EK Success Ltd.

Materials
Card stock: light green, Curious Iridescent shimmery
Sultry printed papers: Vogue, Smart
Kim Hughes stamp sets: Bloomin' Beautiful, Bold Curls, Silhouette Blooms II
Ink: spring green distress; light green and black dye
Markers
12 inches ⅜-inch-wide pink satin ribbon
Magnetic card closure
1⅜-inch circle punch
Artist's watercolor brush
Paper adhesive
Jewel glue

Love

DESIGN BY **SHARON M. REINHART**

Project Note

Adhere elements using glue stick or double-sided tape unless instructed otherwise.

Accordion-fold Card

1 Cut three 7¾ x 3⅞-inch pieces of light tan card stock. Score each piece vertically 3⅞ inches from left edge; fold in half.

2 Unfold card stock; lay two pieces flat, end to end. Lay third piece on top, overlapping first

Materials

Card stock: light tan, shimmery white
Printed paper: ivory/metallic gold, ivory/ metallic gold Maruyama plaid
Lightweight cardboard or 2 square cardboard coasters
Tan gift wrap
Heavy white vellum
2 (1-inch) white card-stock tags
Rubber stamps: square tiles, mini envelope, 2-inch heart, love sentiments, script
Ink pads: embossing, brown or black dye
Gold metallic embossing powder
Gold mini brads
¹⁄₁₆-inch hole punch
Embossing heat tool
Glue stick or double-sided tape
Adhesive foam tape

two pieces; adhere panels where they overlap. Fold accordion-style.

Covers

1 Cut two 5-inch squares from tan gift wrap. Crumple squares for texture; smooth out.

2 Cut two 4-inch squares from lightweight cardboard, or trim cardboard coasters to size.

3 *Front cover:* Cut a 2⅜-inch square window in center of one cardboard square. Cover frame with one of the crumpled squares of gift wrap, folding excess paper to back and adhering on reverse side.

4 Cut a 3¼-inch square of Maruyama plaid; center and adhere to reverse side of front cover. Center and adhere front cover to first panel of card.

5 *Back cover:* Cover remaining cardboard square with remaining square of gift wrap, folding excess paper to back and adhering on reverse side. Center and adhere to last panel of card.

Embellishments

1 Stamp two mini envelopes onto ivory/metallic gold printed paper using dye ink; cut out and fold along assembly lines. Referring to photo throughout, fold ivory envelope flap backward onto printed side of envelope. Punch ¹⁄₁₆-inch hole through envelope and flap; attach mini brad. Repeat with second envelope.

2 Stamp two tiles onto heavy vellum using embossing ink; sprinkle with embossing powder and heat to emboss. Tap off excess. Trim around embossed images. Tuck a tile into the top of each mini envelope; adhere to front cover as shown.

3 Stamp two hearts onto shimmery white card stock using embossing ink; sprinkle with embossing powder and heat to emboss. Tap off excess. Trim around embossed images.

4 Stamp love sentiments onto card-stock tags using embossing ink; sprinkle with embossing powder and heat to emboss. Tap off excess.

5 Attach one tag to one heart with mini brad; using adhesive foam tape, adhere heart to front cover as shown.

6 *Inside card:* Stamp script onto shimmery white card stock using embossing ink; sprinkle with embossing powder and heat to emboss. Tap off excess. Tear a 2½ x 3-inch piece from embossed card stock; adhere to desired panel inside card.

7 Center and adhere a 2½-inch square of Marayuma plaid to embossed card stock.

8 Adhere second tag to remaining heart; center and adhere to Marayuma plaid. ❇

Sources: Marayuma plaid printed paper and heart stamp from Magenta Rubber Stamps; mini envelope and tiles stamps from Quietfire Design; script and sentiments stamps from Hero Arts.

You Can Do It!

DESIGN BY **KATHLEEN PANEITZ**

1 Cut a 4¾ x 20½-inch piece of card stock, piecing together smaller pieces as needed. Score card stock horizontally 5 inches, 10 inches, 13 inches, 16¼ inches and 18½ inches from top, creating card with six panels.

2 Fold top panel down to back; fold remaining panels accordion-style. Counting from the top, panels 1, 3 and 5 will face the back; panels 2, 4 and 6 will face front.

3 Referring to photo throughout, adhere off-white/black pin-dot printed paper to panel 2; trim edges even. With panel 1 folded back, punch through both layers to round off upper corners of panel 2 and adjacent corners of panel 1.

Materials

Beige card stock
Printed papers: off-white with black pin dots, off-white with red "wallpaper" print
Red bird journaling die-cut card
Chipboard die cuts: black 4½-inch brackets, 2-inch black/white pin-dot flower; 3¼-inch black flourish; 3½-inch gray/black/white "Remember" tag
Black "you can do it" rub-on transfer
Black-and-white chipboard buttons: 2 (1-inch), 1 (¾-inch)
⅝-inch red button
Wiggly eye
3 inches ½-inch-wide black-and-white gingham-check ribbon
Embroidery floss: red, white
Needle
Corner rounder
Paper adhesive

4 Adhere chipboard bracket to top of panel 2. Embellish panel with "Remember" tag and flower as shown. Thread white floss through holes in red button; adhere button in center of flower.

5 Sew black-and-white buttons to bird die-cut card using red floss; adhere wiggly eye to bird. Adhere bird card to panel 4 as shown. Apply "you can do it" rub-on transfer to panel to left of bird.

6 Adhere off-white/red printed paper to panel 6; trim edges even. With panel 5 folded back against panel 6, punch through both layers to round off lower corners of panel 6 and adjacent corners of panel 5.

7 Adhere chipboard bracket to bottom of panel 6. Tie ribbon around chipboard flourish as shown; trim ends at an angle and adhere flourish to panel 6. ✹

Sources: Printed papers, Jigsaw Pieces chipboard embellishments and chipboard buttons from Making Memories; bird die-cut card from Jenni Bowlin Studio; rub-on tranfser from Scenic Route Paper Co.

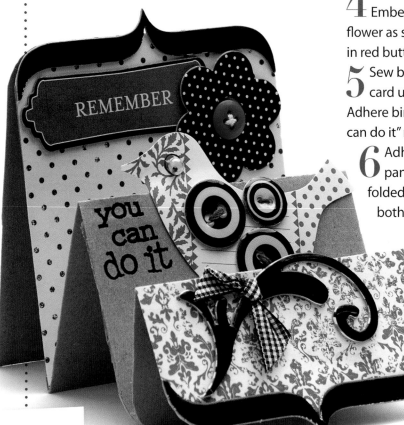

Love You

DESIGN BY **KATHLEEN PANEITZ**

1 Form a 4¾ x 4¾-inch top-folded card from black card stock; round corners using corner rounder punch.

2 Center and adhere square floral card-stock die-cut from Floral 1 sheet to card front; apply rub-on transfer to center of die cut.

3 Referring to photo throughout, connect oval "If you only knew" and round "you rock my world" die cuts from So in Love sheet to card front using flip-flop fasteners so that die cuts will open accordion-style.

4 Cut a 4⅛-inch circle from black card stock; adhere to reverse side of round die cut.

5 Adhere chipboard scalloped circle to oval die cut; adhere chipboard heart to round die cut.

6 Punch a ¼-inch hole near left edge of round die cut. Make a reinforcing ring by first punching a ¼-inch hole from black card stock, then punching a ½-inch circle around it to form ring. Adhere ring to round die cut around punched hole.

7 Fold ribbon in half. Thread folded end through hole, then thread ends through loop; tighten gently and trim ribbon ends. ✹

Sources: Jotters from Luxe Designs; Jigsaw Shapes chipboard embellishments from Making Memories; rub-on transfer from Lasting Impressions; ribbon from Mrs. Grossman's; flip-flop fasteners from Destination Scrapbook Designs.

Materials

Black card stock
Jotters card-stock die-cut sheets: So in Love, Floral 1
Chipboard die cuts: 2⅛-inch black-and-white scalloped circle with heart, 1-inch black heart
Black "love you" rub-on transfer
3 tiny orange rhinestones
6 inches ½-inch-wide black-and-white striped ribbon
Circle cutter
Punches: corner rounder, ½-inch hole, ¼-inch hole
Flip-flop fasteners
Paper adhesive

Holiday Joy

DESIGN BY **MELANIE DOUTHIT**

1 Cut a 12 x 5¾-inch piece of dark red card stock. Score card stock vertically 4 and 8 inches from left edge. Fold panels accordion-style.

2 Trim top corners of each panel to form matching tag shapes.

Card Front

1 Referring to photo throughout, adhere Peppermint Stick printed paper to card front; trim edges even. Center and adhere a 1¾ x 5¾-inch strip of O Christmas Tree printed paper to card front.

2 Stamp Christmas tree onto light green card stock; round corners using corner rounder punch. Adhere stamped image to dark red card stock; trim, leaving ⅛-inch borders. Center and adhere to card ⅛ inch from bottom edge.

3 Above stamped image, adhere Park Buddies alphabet stickers to spell "joy."

Inner Panels

1 *Left:* Adhere Let It Snow printed paper to panel; trim edges even. Center and adhere a 1½ x 5½-inch strip of Holly Jolly printed paper to panel. Using Chalkboard Alpha Black stickers, assemble "Wishing" and "You" on Angels Sing printed paper; trim around words and adhere to panel as shown. Add Holiday Gifts stickers as desired.

2 *Center:* Adhere Star Bright printed paper to panel; trim edges even. Embellish with ½-inch-wide strips cut from a complementary portion of Holly Jolly printed paper. Using Chalkboard Alpha Black stickers, assemble "A Very Merry" on Angels Sing printed paper; trim around words and adhere to red card stock. Trim card stock along top and sides, leaving narrow borders; tear card stock across bottom edge. Adhere to panel as shown.

3 *Right:* Adhere Angels Sing printed paper to panel; trim edges even. Stamp "Christmas" across top of a 2⅝ x 3⅝-inch piece of light green card stock; adhere red paper rickrack below words. Adhere card stock to Peppermint Stick printed paper; trim, leaving ¼-inch borders. Center and adhere "Christmas" panel to card as shown; embellish with Holiday Gifts stickers.

Finishing

1 Using zigzag stitch, machine-stitch around card front close to edge.

2 Adhere red paper rickrack vertically to card front ⅜ inch from right edge.

3 Center and punch a ¼-inch hole through card front near top edge; thread ribbon through hole and knot. Trim notches in ribbon ends. ✻

Sources: Printed papers and Holiday Gifts stickers from Flair Designs; stickers from SEI (Park Buddies) and Jenni Bowlin (Chalkboard Alpha Black); paper rickrack from Doodlebug Design; See D's stamps from Darice Inc.; Zip Dry Paper Glue from Beacon Adhesives Inc.

Materials

Card stock: red, dark red, light green
Printed papers: Peppermint Stick, Holly Jolly Stripe, Let It Snow, Star Bright, Angels Sing, O Christmas Tree
Card-stock stickers: Park Buddies, Chalkboard Alpha Black, Holiday Gifts
Red paper rickrack
Christmas No. 50952 stamp set
Moss green ink
6 inches 1-inch-wide green-and-white striped grosgrain ribbon
Punches: corner rounder, ¼-inch hole punch
Sewing machine with white thread
Instant-dry paper glue

Cupcake Celebration

DESIGN BY **LINDSEY BOTKIN**

Project Note

Adhere elements using paper adhesive unless instructed otherwise.

Cut a 9¾ x 4¾-inch piece of blue card stock. Score card stock vertically 3¼ x 6½ inches from left edge; close card accordion-style. Referring to photo throughout, round off opposite corners using corner rounder punch.

Front Panel

1 Cut a 3 x 4½-inch piece of Gravity printed card stock; round off corners to match card panel. Center and adhere printed card stock to card.

2 Cut a 2¾ x 4¼-inch piece of Reaction printed card stock. Round off corners; center and adhere printed paper to card.

3 Cut a 2¾ x 3-inch piece of white card stock. Stamp stars onto card stock; color orange with markers. Center and adhere stamped paper to card.

4 Stamp cupcake onto white card stock; color with markers and cut out. Center and adhere cupcake to card with adhesive foam dots. Stamp "Celebrate!" on lower right corner of panel.

5 *Tab:* Cut a 1 x ½-inch piece of orange card stock; round off upper left corner using corner rounder punch. Center and attach eyelet; knot ribbon through eyelet. Adhere tab at upper left corner as shown.

Center Panel

1 Cut a 3 x 4½-inch piece of orange card stock; stamp with stars. Round off corners to match panel of card. Center and adhere card stock to card.

2 Cut a 1¼ x 4¼-inch piece of Reaction printed card stock; adhere to card close to left edge.

3 Stamp "best wishes" onto white card stock; cut rectangle around words, then round off upper corners using corner rounder punch. Adhere to card as shown.

Materials

Printed card stock: Gravity, Reaction
Card stock: orange, blue, white
Clear stamp sets: Cupcakes, All Occasions
Black ink
Markers
4 silver eyelets
¼-inch blue ribbon with green stitching
Eyelet-setting tool
Corner rounder
Adhesive foam dots
Paper adhesive

4 Stamp a cupcake onto white card stock; color with markers and cut out. Adhere cupcake to card with adhesive foam dots as shown.

5 Attach three silver eyelets, evenly spaced, below "best wishes" panel.

Back Panel

1 Cut a 3 x 4½-inch piece of Gravity printed card stock; round off corners to match front panel of card. Center and adhere printed card stock to card.

2 Cut a 2¾ x 4¼-inch piece of Reaction printed card stock; round off corners. Tie ribbon around card stock, knotting ends on front; center and adhere card stock to card.

3 Stamp cupcakes onto white card stock; color with markers, then trim around cupcakes to make a strip 2¾ inches long. Adhere stamped card stock to orange card stock; trim, leaving narrow borders. Adhere cupcakes to card 1 inch from bottom. ✺

Sources: Printed card stock from Crate Paper; stamp sets from Inkadinkado; Copic markers from Copic.

Thinking of You

DESIGN BY **LINDSEY BOTKIN**

1 Cut a 10 x 3¾-inch piece of card stock. Score card stock vertically 2½ inches, 5 inches and 7½ inches from left edge; fold card accordion-style. Round off corners using corner rounder punch. Lightly ink edges and folds with black.

2 Stamp images on card panels using black ink. Color and outline images using colored inks and blender pen.

3 Attach eyelet in upper left corner of front panel. Knot ribbon through eyelet; trim ribbon ends. ✹

Sources: Stamp sets from Inkadinkado; solvent-based ink from Tsukineko Inc.; blender pen from Stampin' Up!

Materials

Off-white card stock
Clear stamp sets: Garden Flower, Thinking of You
Ink: black solvent-based, orange, yellow, pink, light blue, light green
Blender pen
Silver eyelet
Eyelet-setting tool
¼-inch-wide olive green ribbon with off-white stitches
Corner rounder

FABULOUS FOLDS FOR CARD MAKING

Snowflake Accordion

DESIGN BY **ROBIN ARNOLD**

1 Copy pattern from page 170. Tape vellum to pattern using removable tape. Lay pattern and vellum on embossing mat. Rub waxed paper over vellum to make embossing easier.

2 Trace border lines and snowflakes using small ball embossing tool.

3 Turn vellum over; tape on top of pattern. Place on perforating mat. Using 2-needle tool, pierce edges of three large snowflakes where marked on pattern. **Note:** *Insert one needle of tool into the last hole pierced each time to maintain even spacing. Remove pattern.*

4 *Cut along perforated line:* Insert scissors into one perforated hole and twist scissors slightly to the left while cutting to cut a tiny triangle. **Note:** *You may want to practice on scrap vellum first.*

5 Referring to photo throughout, fold vellum accordion-style along fold lines, taking care not to fold the large snowflakes.

6 Fold card stock identically to vellum; layer card stock under vellum.

7 Open card stock and vellum; lay both pieces on perforating mat. Using 2-needle tool, pierce edges of three large snowflakes where marked on pattern. **Note:** *Insert one needle of tool into the last hole pierced each time to maintain even spacing. Remove card stock.*

8 Place vellum and pattern on embossing mat. Using small ball tool, 4-needle tool and star tool, complete embossing according to pattern.

9 Remove vellum. Cut all crosses and along border on both vellum and card stock. To cut crosses: Insert tips of scissors into two holes farthest from you. Twist slightly to the left as you cut. Turn vellum between the next two holes. Repeat until cross is completed. **Note:** *You may want to practice on scrap vellum first.*

Materials
Blue card stock
24-pound white iridescent vellum
Waxed paper
Small ball embossing tool
Perforating tools: 2-needle, 4-needle
Star tool
Small, sharp scissors with fine point, such as scherrenschnitte scissors
Mats: embossing, perforating
Removable tape
Vellum tape

10 Using vellum tape, attach vellum to card stock along folds. ❋

Sources: Chatham Inclusions vellum and Pergamano tools and mats from Marco's Paper.

TEA BAG FOLDS

Originating from an origami technique, tea bag folding is a must-try for young and old alike. Start with papers intended specifically for tea bag fold projects, or create your own papers with rubber-stamped designs. Easy-to-follow diagrams will make creating these projects a breeze.

Tea bag folding traveled to the United States from Europe, but its origins are linked to unit origami, paper folding practiced in Asia for centuries.

Both start with a simple square of lightweight paper, carefully and precisely folded.

Individual folded squares are combined with other squares folded the same way. The resulting motif resembles a kaleidoscope, flower or geometric design that is flat enough to add to a card and send through the mail.

Tea bag folding, like origami, is portable, easy to learn, and requires little in the way of tools and supplies. Children catch on quickly, and enthusiasts will find that tea bag folding will hold their interest for many years.

As you've probably guessed, tea bag folding got its name from the decorative lightweight papers that were used when the craft took root— the packets that held a tea bag. Cut into squares, the paper was the right size and weight, and the designs were colorful and interesting.

Think of a flower with five petals. Now envision one that has nine. Tea bag folded shapes, like flowers, can be simple or complex, incorporating just a few folded squares within a motif, or many. These motifs interlock; they overlap—the possibilities are endless.

Teabag Folding 2, from Search Press, is just one of the many books of tea bag folding papers that are available.

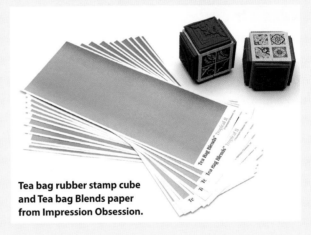

Tea bag rubber stamp cube and Tea bag Blends paper from Impression Obsession.

Choosing Papers

Choosing paper is a big part of the fun. Papers printed with squares, ready to cut apart, are a good way to start. These papers are available by the sheet or in books. You can also use rubber stamps or computer graphics to create your own.

The key is using durable but lightweight papers that will hold nice, crisp folds. It's important to be able to repeat the same unit over and over so that the completed motifs have a precise elegance, very important to tea bag folding. Asian papers are the perfect weight and are usually high quality.

Many preprinted papers have small scenes or pictures, flowers and leaves or geometric designs that look very different depending on how the papers are folded. Some papers are two-sided, another way to add variety and pizzazz to a card.

Getting Started

To insure the most success with your tea bag fold projects, begin by practicing the folds for the Basic Square and Basic Triangle. Now

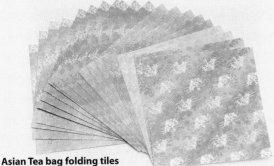

Asian Tea bag folding tiles from Toyo Corporation available from Michaels.

practice some more. It may take a while before your fingers get the hang of it. Don't give up! If you were learning to play golf, you wouldn't think you had to be proficient after the first basket of balls, and tea bag folding is much easier than golf.

You'll find each new pattern easier than the one before, even if it's a more complicated pattern. Once you understand how to use the diagrams and your tools, you'll be ready to make cards embellished with tea bag folded shapes for any occasion.

The tools are minimal: bone folder, craft knife, straight edge and cutting mat.

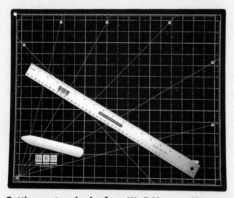

Cutting mat and ruler from We R Memory Keepers.

The supplies are equally minimal: paper and a pattern, a bit of glue or double-stick tape. If you buy precut papers, you don't even need the knife, ruler and mat.

The bone folder is invaluable. Even if you have long fingernails, use the bone folder to get those crisp creases! (It won't leave shiny marks on the paper the way your fingernails would.)

Making Cards

Consider several tea bag folded motifs scattered on a card front like snowflakes—or lined up like flowers, with stems made of wire or ribbon. Add a single motif to a card-stock square. Layer the motif onto a card front. Simple or complicated, jazzy or serene, tea bag folding and the cards you'll make with the motifs you've created offer a lifetime of possibilities.

Basic Square

Fold paper square in half, wrong sides facing, vertically, horizontally and diagonally in both directions; unfold (Fig. 1).

Turn folded square on the diagonal (Fig. 2).

Fold square in half again, wrong sides facing, on the diagonal. Push sides to inside along folded edge (Fig. 3).

Completed Basic Square looks like Fig. 4.

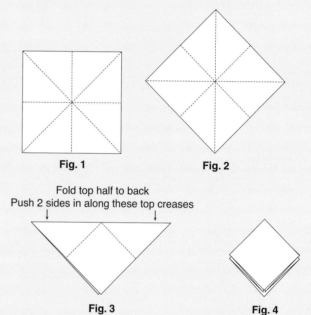

Basic Triangle

Fold paper square in half, wrong sides facing, vertically, horizontally and diagonally in both directions; unfold (Fig. 1).

Fold square in half again, wrong sides facing, along horizontal fold. Push sides to inside along folded edge (Fig. 2).

Completed Basic Triangle looks like Fig. 3. ✺

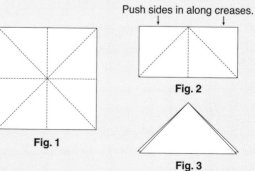

Happy Birthday

DESIGN BY **MELANIE DOUTHIT**

Materials

Card stock: light blue textured,
    pink coral solid
Printed paper: Fairy Godmother, Happily
    Ever After
Rubber stamps: Monarch #52001,
    Birthday #50432
Blue ink pad
⅜-inch light blue rhinestone
    decorative brad
Threading water punch
Paper adhesive

Tea Bag Folded Medallion

1 Cut eight 2-inch squares from Happily Ever After printed paper. Referring to diagrams and instructions, page 110, fold each into a Basic Triangle.

2 Arrange triangles in a medallion, interlocking triangles as shown (Figs. 1–3), and adhering triangles to each other where they overlap with paper adhesive.

Assembly

1 Form a 5½ x 4¼-inch top-folded card from light blue card stock.

2 Cut a 5⅜ x 4-inch piece of pink coral solid card stock; center and adhere to card front.

3 Cut a 5⅛ x 4-inch piece of Fairy Godmother printed paper; trim bottom edge using threading water punch, then center and adhere to card front.

4 Cut a 5⅛ x 2¼-inch strip from white card stock and a 5⅛ x 2¾-inch strip from Happily Ever After printed paper. Center and adhere Happily Ever After strip to card front; center and adhere white card-stock strip to Happily Ever After printed paper.

5 Attach rhinestone brad to center of tea bag folded medallion; adhere medallion to white card-stock strip ½ inch from left edge of card.

6 Stamp "Happy Birthday" and butterfly onto white card stock to right of medallion as shown. ✹

Sources: Cinderella printed paper from Piggy Tales; stamps from Inque Boutique/Darice Inc.; brad from Deja Views; punch from Fiskars.

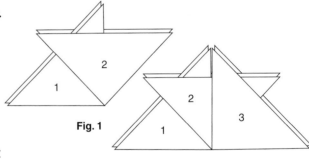

Fig. 1

Fig. 2

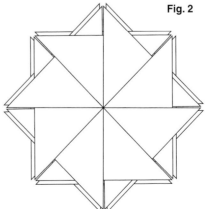

Fig. 3

Grateful Tulips

DESIGN BY **JULIE EBERSOLE**

Project Note
Adhere elements using paper adhesive unless instructed otherwise.

Tea Bag Folded Tulips

1 Cut three 2-inch squares from origami paper. Form each into a tulip as follows:

2 Position paper square on the diagonal, printed side down. Fold square on the diagonal, wrong sides facing; position fold at bottom (Fig. 1).

3 Fold up corners at sides to form tulip (Fig. 2).

Assembly

1 Form a 4½ x 5½-inch top-folded card from gold card stock.

2 Cut a 3¼ x 4½-inch piece of red card stock; adhere to white card stock. Trim very close to edge of white card stock using decorative-edge scissors; center and adhere card-stock panel to card front.

3 Cut stems from ribbon, one each 3⅛ inches, 2⅛ inches and 1⅞ inches. Referring to photo throughout, adhere ribbon stems to red card stock; adhere tea bag folded tulips to card at top of stems.

4 Cut a 2⅞ x 9⁄16-inch strip from white card stock. Stamp "with Gratitude" in center of strip; punch a hole in each end of strip. Cut two 3-inch pieces from remaining ribbon. Knot one length through each hole; trim ribbon ends. Center and adhere stamped panel to card front 1⅛ inches from bottom using adhesive foam squares. ❋

Sources: Rubber stamp from All Night Media; ribbon from May Arts.

Materials
Card stock: gold, red, white
Gold/red/white floral origami paper
"with Gratitude" rubber stamp
Rose red dye ink
14 inches ³⁄16-inch-wide green ribbon with white stitches
⅛-inch hole punch
Decorative-edge scissors
Double-sided tape
Adhesive foam squares

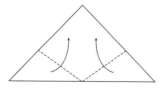

Fig. 1

Fig. 2

The Scoop

DESIGN BY **KATHLEEN PANEITZ**

Materials
White card stock
Printed paper: Floral Stripes, Eclectique
   Scroll
Delaney "the scoop" journaling tag
⅝-inch decorative button
Yellow scrapbooking floss
Paper adhesive

Tea Bag Folded Motif

1 Cut four 2-inch squares from Eclectique Scroll printed paper.

2 Referring to instructions and diagrams, page 110, fold each square into a Basic Triangle with turquoise side facing out.

3 Referring to diagrams and instructions for Grateful Tulips, page 112, fold each Basic Triangle into a tulip shape measuring 1⅛ inches wide at its widest point.

4 Referring to photo throughout, adhere tulips to journaling tag with points meeting in center.

Assembly

1 Form a 5 x 5-inch top-folded card from white card stock.

2 Adhere Floral Stripe printed paper to card front; trim edges even. If desired, cut a ¾ x 5-inch accent strip from contrasting portion of printed paper; adhere to card front along left edge.

3 Adhere journaling tag with folded motif to white card stock; trim, leaving very narrow borders. Adhere panel to card ⁹⁄₁₆ inch from right edge.

4 Thread floss through button; tie ends in a bow on front. Center and adhere button to folded motif. ✻

Sources: Sunrise Smoothie printed paper (Floral Stripe) from Cloud 9 Design; Eclectique Scroll printed paper from Chatterbox; Noteworthy II journaling tag from Making Memories; Softies button from KI Memories.

Flower Fold Card

DESIGN BY **SHARON M. REINHART**

Project Note
Adhere elements using paper adhesive unless instructed otherwise.

Tea Bag Folded Flower

1 Cut five 2-inch squares from printed paper. Referring to instructions and diagrams on page 110, fold each into a Basic Triangle.

2 Position each triangle on point as shown in Fig. 1 and fold as follows:

3 Working with top layer only, fold over left side (Fig. 2) until outer edge aligns with vertical center (Fig. 3). Repeat on opposite side (Fig. 4).

4 Referring to photo throughout, slide three folded shapes together to form main flower, sliding edges between layers of adjacent folded piece as shown. Turn flower wrong side up; secure with double-sided tape.

Assembly

1 Form a 5½ x 4¼-inch top-folded card from lime card stock.

2 Cut a 3¼-inch square from printed-paper; cut a 3-inch square from lime card stock. Center and adhere card-stock square to printed paper square; center and adhere squares to card front.

3 Referring to photo throughout, adhere remaining folded motifs in lower corners of card, edges even.

Materials
Lime card stock
Lime green floral printed paper
Silver metallic peel-off stickers: stem with leaves, ³⁄₁₆-inch dot
Double-sided tape
Paper adhesive
Foam mounting tape

4 Adhere Tea Bag Folded Flower to center card-stock square with foam mounting tape.

5 Adhere stem-and-leaves sticker to card; adhere dot sticker to flower at base of petals. ✹

Sources: Printed paper from Doodlebug Design Inc.; stickers from Magenta.

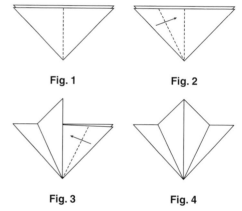

Fig. 1   Fig. 2

Fig. 3   Fig. 4

Folded Flakes Card

DESIGN BY **SHARON M. REINHART**

Project Note
Adhere elements using paper adhesive unless instructed otherwise.

Tea Bag Folded Snowflake

1 Cut eight 2-inch squares from printed paper. Referring to instructions and diagrams on page 110, fold each into a Basic Triangle.

2 Referring to steps 2 and 3 of instructions and diagrams for the Tea Bag Folded Flower for Flower Fold Card, page 114, fold each Basic Triangle.

3 Referring to photo throughout, slide folded shapes together to form snowflake, sliding edges between layers of adjacent folded pieces as shown. Turn motif wrong side up; secure with double-sided tape.

Materials
Card stock: white, blue shimmer
Blue/white snowflakes printed paper
¼-inch clear rhinestone
Die cutter
Nestabilities Classic Scalloped Oval Large #2918 die
Double-sided tape
Paper adhesive
Foam mounting tape

Assembly

1 Form a 5½ x 4¼-inch top-folded card from blue shimmer card stock.

2 Using die cutter and die, die-cut and emboss a 4½ x 3⅜-inch oval from white card stock; center and adhere to card front.

3 Center and adhere snowflake to oval with foam mounting tape.

4 Adhere rhinestone in center of snowflake. ✺

Sources: Printed paper from Paper Pizzazz; Nestabilities die-cutting machine and die from Spellbinder Paper Arts.

In Triplicate

DESIGN BY **SHARON M. REINHART**

Project Note
Adhere elements using paper adhesive unless instructed otherwise.

Tea Bag Folded Medallion

1 Stamp square motif 16 times onto olive paper using black ink, re-inking stamp each time; trim around squares.

2 Referring to instructions and diagrams on page 110, fold 10 stamped squares into Basic Triangles.

3 Referring to diagrams on page 117, fold each Basic Triangle as shown.

4 Referring to photo throughout, slide eight shapes together to form central medallion, applying small pieces of double-sided tape to sides of folded motifs and sliding edges between layers of adjacent folded pieces as shown. Turn medallion wrong side up; secure with tape.

Assembly

1 Form a 5½ x 4¼-inch top-folded card from black card stock.

2 Cut two 1⅝-inch squares of black card stock. Ink desired side of faux finish cube stamp with embossing ink; stamp onto center of each card-stock square, re-inking stamp between impressions. Immediately sprinkle stamped designs with embossing powder; tap off excess and heat to emboss.

3 Center and adhere an unfolded stamped olive square to each embossed square.

4 Fold the four remaining unfolded olive squares in half on the diagonal. Center and adhere three squares over the top fold of the card, overlapping slightly as needed. Center and adhere the remaining folded square over the bottom of card front.

5 Center and adhere embossed, stamped squares point to point on card front as shown. Center and adhere folded motif to card front over stamped, embossed squares using foam mounting tape. Attach rhinestone in center of folded motif using adhesive dot.

6 Adhere remaining folded motifs in lower corners of card front, edges even. ✺

Sources: Printed paper from Magenta; stamps from Paper Parachute (square motif) and Stampendous (Quad Cube).

Materials
Black card stock
Olive Odyssey printed paper
Rubber stamps: square motif #W-523,
   Faux Finish Quad Cube #TC52
Ink: black, embossing
Gold embossing powder
Topaz rhinestone
Embossing heat tool
Double-sided tape
Paper adhesive
Foam mounting tape
Adhesive dot

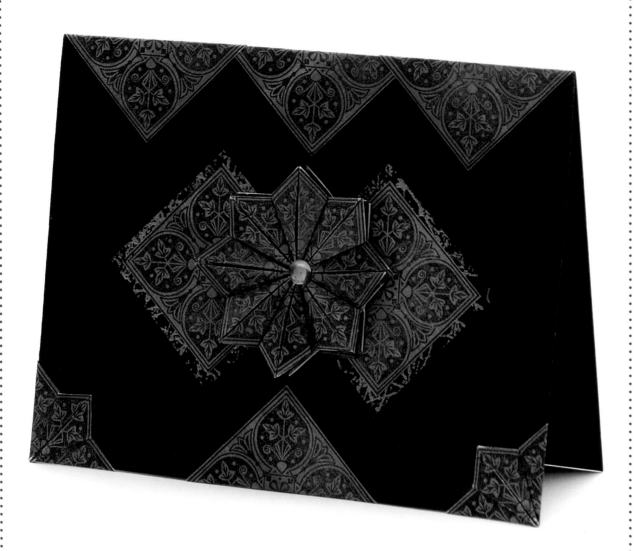

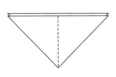

Fig. 1

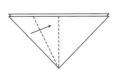

Fig. 2

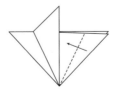

Fig. 3

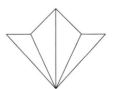

Fig. 4

Elegance

DESIGN BY **SHARON M. REINHART**

Project Note

Adhere elements using double-sided tape unless instructed otherwise.

1 Cut a 2¾ x 2-inch piece of black card stock.

2 Stamp square motif 10 times onto light sage paper; trim around squares.

3 Fold two squares in half diagonally, wrong sides facing. Adhere over shorter ends of black card stock.

4 Referring to instructions and diagrams, page 110, fold six of the remaining stamped squares into Basic Triangles. Fold each Basic Triangle as follows:

5 Working with front layer only, fold and tuck right point up and under until point meets point at center top of triangle and edge meets vertical center fold (Fig. 1). Repeat on opposite side (Fig. 2). When piece is folded, a small square will remain on front.

6 Turn four folded pieces wrong side up; align pieces edge to edge to form square (Fig. 3). Secure with tape. Flip over; smaller squares will form larger square in center (Fig. 4). Center and adhere folded motif to black card-stock panel on the diagonal.

7 Adhere remaining folded pieces adjacent to left and right edges of central motif and over paper squares attached in step 3.

Assembly

1 Form a 4¼ x 5½-inch side-folded card from dark green card stock.

2 Cut a 2 x 2½-inch piece of light green card stock; adhere to card front 5/16 inch from right and bottom edges.

Materials
Card stock: black, dark sage
Light sage printed paper
1 7/16-inch square motif rubber stamp
Black ink
3 black mini brads
Paper piercer
Double-sided tape
Foam mounting tape

3 Using foam mounting squares, adhere black card stock with folded motifs to card as shown, 9/16 inch from right and bottom edges.

4 Punch a vertical row of three evenly spaced holes ½ inch from right edge and beginning 5/8 inch from top; attach mini brads.

5 Adhere remaining stamped motifs inside card, adhering one over ends of mini brads. ❋

Sources: Printed paper from Anna Griffin Inc.; rubber stamp from Paper Parachute.

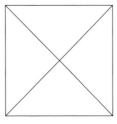

Fig. 1

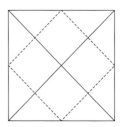

Fig. 2

Fig. 3

Fig. 4

Kick Up Your Heels

DESIGN BY **KATHLEEN PANEITZ**

Tea Bag Folded Motif

1 Cut eight 1½-inch squares from polka-dot printed paper.

2 Referring to instructions and diagrams, page 110, fold each square into a Basic Triangle.

3 Cut a 3¼-inch square of blue weave printed paper; round off corners using corner rounder punch. Referring to photo throughout, apply "Congratulations" rub-on transfer to upper right corner.

4 Referring to Figs.1–4, arrange triangles in a circle, overlapping triangles as shown and leaving a 1-inch opening in center. Adhere triangles to one another where they overlap; center and adhere circle of triangles to blue weave printed-paper panel.

5 Cut a 3⁷⁄₁₆-inch square of white card stock; round off corners using corner rounder punch. Center and adhere panel with folded stars to white card stock.

6 Apply star rub-on transfer to brad; attach brad to card stock in center of triangles.

Assembly

1 Adhere blue weave printed paper to large tag; trim edges even.

Materials

White card stock
4½ x 6¼-inch cream card-stock library pocket card with tag
Giggle Boy printed paper: polka dots, stripes, blue weave
"Y" play tag
Black rub-on transfers: "kick up your heels," "Congratulations," 1-inch star
1-inch blue striped decorative brad
6 inches ½-inch-wide dark green/white polka-dot ribbon
Punches: corner rounder, ¼-inch hole
Paper adhesive

2 Adhere "Y" tag to center top of tag with top edges even. Center and punch a ¼-inch hole through tags near top edge; knot ribbon through hole and trim ends at an angle.

3 Cut a 4½ x 4⅛-inch piece of striped printed paper; adhere to front of library pocket with side and bottom edges even.

4 Apply "kick up your heels" rub-on transfer to cream card stock margin along top edge of pocket front.

5 Tuck tag into pocket. Adhere panel with folded triangles to pocket ¼ inch from right and bottom edges. ✳

Sources: Library pocket card from Crafts Etc.; printed paper and "Y" tag from Sweetwater; rub-on transfers from Scenic Route Paper Co.; brad from Stemma.

Fig. 1

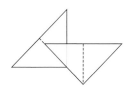

Fig. 2

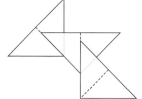

Fig. 3

Fig. 4

Birthday Wrap

DESIGN BY **JULIE EBERSOLE**

A VERY HAPPY BIRTHDAY

Project note: Adhere elements using double-sided tape unless instructed otherwise.

Tea Bag Folded Motif

1 Cut eight 2-inch squares from cream printed paper. Referring to instructions and diagrams, page 110, fold each piece into a Basic Square. Referring to Figs. 1–3, fold each square as follows:

2 Working with only the top layer of the square, fold the left edge under (Fig. 1) until the outer edge touches the vertical fold in center of square (Fig. 2). Repeat on right side (Fig. 3). Referring to photo throughout, assemble folded shapes into a medallion:

3 Slide back layer on side of one shape between front and back layers of another shape until kite-shaped sections on front lie edge to edge; secure with dot of paper adhesive. Repeat to attach remaining pieces and complete the motif.

4 Adhere medallion to 1¼-inch circle punched or cut from card stock.

Assembly

1 Form a 4¼ x 5½-inch side-folded card from vanilla card stock.

2 Cut a 4 x 5¼-inch piece of Letters printed paper; center and adhere to card front.

3 Closure band: Lay a sheet of pink/cream floral printed paper right side up with longer edges at top and bottom. Score paper vertically ¾ inch from left edge, then ¼ inch from first scored line, ¾ inch from second scored line, ¼ inch from third, and so on until the entire sheet is scored. Fold paper into pleats along scored lines.

4 Cut two 3-inch-wide strips from pleated paper; adhere ends to form a single long strip. Wrap pleated strip around card; adhere ends to each other—not to card—where they overlap on reverse side.

5 Cut a 9½ x 1¼-inch strip from multicolored floral printed paper; adhere to cream printed

paper. Trim cream paper very close to edge of floral paper using decorative-edge scissors. Center and adhere strip to pleated strip, wrapping ends around to reverse side and adhering.

6 Stamp sentiment onto white vellum; trim tag shape around words.

7 Pierce center of tea bag folded medallion using paper piercer; attach brad. Adhere end of tag to reverse side of medallion as shown; center and adhere medallion to floral printed-paper strip on card front. ✽

Sources: Printed papers from Penny Black (Script) and Anna Griffin Inc.; Anna Griffin "A Very Happy Birthday" stamp set from Plaid Enterprises Inc./All Night Media; brad from K&Company.

Materials

Vanilla card stock
Printed paper: Letters, cream, pink/cream floral, multicolored floral
White heavyweight vellum
"Happy birthday" stamp
Dark brown chalk ink
Pearl decorative brad
Paper piercer or large needle
1¼-inch circle punch (optional)
Decorative-edge scissors
Paper adhesive
Double-sided tape

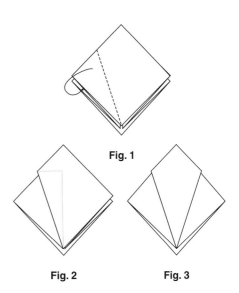

Fig. 1

Fig. 2   **Fig. 3**

I Love You Card

DESIGN BY **SHARON M. REINHART**

Project Note
Adhere elements using glue stick unless instructed otherwise.

Tea Bag Folded Motif

1 Cut six 2-inch squares from Chyogami paper. Referring to Figs. 1–3, fold each piece into a Basic Square.

2 Working with only the top layer of the square, fold the left edge under (Fig. 4) until the outer edge touches the vertical fold in center of square (Fig. 5). Repeat on right side (Fig. 6). Referring to photo throughout, assemble folded shapes into a medallion.

3 Referring to photo throughout, slide together three folded motifs to make one half of the

central design (Fig. 7): Slide back layer on side of one shape between front and back layers of another shape until kite-shaped sections on front lie edge to edge; secure with glue stick. Repeat to attach a third folded shape.

4 Repeat step 3 with remaining folded shapes to form second half of central design.

5 Turn assembled design halves wrong side up; align straight edges and secure with tape.

6 Cut a 2¼-inch-square piece of coral card stock. Center and adhere folded motif to card stock, positioning card stock on the diagonal so that center points at top and bottom of folded motif are outlined by top and bottom corners of card stock.

Assembly

1 Form a 5½-inch-square side-folded card from coral card stock.

2 Cut a 3-inch square of chipboard and a 4-inch square of Chiyogami printed paper. Cover chipboard with Chiyogami paper, wrapping edges neatly to reverse side. Center and adhere chipboard square to card front ½ inch from top.

Materials
Coral card stock
Pink/green/cream floral
  Chiyogami paper
Gold metallic "I [heart] You"
  peel-off sticker
Gold cabochon
Chipboard
Adhesive dots
Glue stick
Double-sided tape

3 Center and adhere folded motif to chipboard square as shown. Adhere cabochon to center of folded motif using adhesive dot.

4 Cut 7 x ¼-inch strip from Chiyogami paper. Adhere across card front ⅞ inch from bottom with left end of strip even with fold; wrap excess around right edge to inside and adhere.

5 Cut a 3 x 1-inch piece of coral card stock; center and adhere sticker to card stock. Center card stock over Chiyogami paper strip as shown and adhere to card front with adhesive dots.

6 Embellish interior of card with paper cutouts as desired. ✺

Source: Chiyogami paper from The Japanese Paper Place.

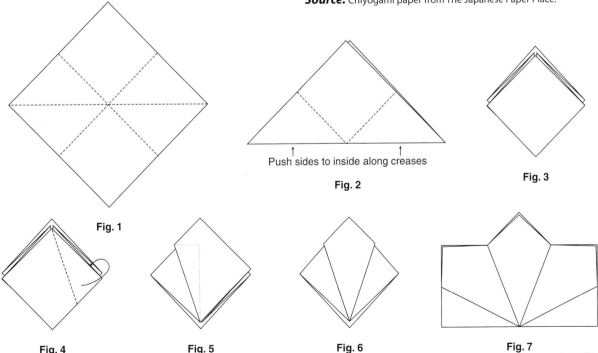

Push sides to inside along creases

Fig. 1

Fig. 2

Fig. 3

Fig. 4

Fig. 5

Fig. 6

Fig. 7

Celebrate

DESIGN BY **LENAE GERIG,** COURTESY OF HOT OFF THE PRESS

Project Note

Adhere elements using glue stick unless instructed otherwise.

Tea Bag Folded Pinwheel

1 Cut six 1½-inch squares from orange circles printed paper and six from orange plaid printed paper from Creative Pack. Fold each square as follows:

2 Position paper square right side down on diagonal. Fold sides in to meet in center (Fig. 1) to form kite shape (Fig. 2).

3 Turn folded shapes seam side down. Referring to photo throughout, overlap folded shapes on a piece of lime green vellum from Creative Pack to form a 3½-inch-diameter pinwheel, alternating circles and plaid patterns.

4 Adhere folded shapes to each other and to vellum using mini glue dots. Trim around pinwheel, leaving a narrow vellum border.

Assembly

1 Trim 1½ inches from one end of card to form a 5-inch-square side-folded card.

2 Cut a 4⅝-inch square of lime green vellum and a 4⅝6-inch square of orange textured printed paper from Creative Pack; center and adhere vellum to card front; center and adhere orange printed paper to vellum.

3 Cut a 2½ x 4¼-inch piece of circles printed paper from Creative Pack; ink edges black, then center and adhere to orange textured printed paper on card front with top and bottom edges even.

4 Center and adhere ribbon across card front using mini glue dots; trim ribbon ends even with edges of card. Center and adhere folded pinwheel to card front using mini glue dots.

5 Cut out "Celebrate" square from Creative Pack; center and adhere to folded pinwheel using adhesive foam tape.

Materials

Cardmaker's 5 x 6½-inch blank white card
Cardmaker's Citrus Creative Pack (includes printed paper and vellum)
5 inches ⅜-inch-wide lime green Cardmaker's Citrus grosgrain ribbon
Cardmaker's Citrus Creative Kit (includes mini brads)
Black ink pad
Glue stick
Adhesive foam tape
Mini glue dots

6 Pierce hole through card front in each corner of orange textured printed paper square; attach orange and lime green mini brads from Creative Kit in holes, alternating colors. ✴

Source: Cardmaker's card, Creative Pack, ribbon and Creative Kit from Hot Off The Press.

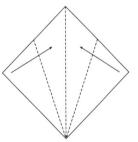

Fig. 1

Fig. 2

Friendship

DESIGN BY **LENAE GERIG,** COURTESY OF HOT OFF THE PRESS

Tea Bag Folded Motif

Project Note
Adhere elements using paper adhesive unless instructed otherwise.

1 Cut eight 1½-inch squares from polka-dot printed paper from Creative Pack. Referring to step 2 of instructions and diagrams for the Tea Bag Folded Pinwheel for Celebrate, page 127, fold each square into a kite shape.

2 Turn folded shapes seam side down. Referring to photo throughout, adhere shapes edge to edge on purple textured paper from Creative Pack. Trim around motif, leaving very narrow purple border.

Assembly

1 Turn card so fold is at top; trim 2 inches from bottom of front flap only. Adhere lavender words printed paper from Creative Pack to card front; trim edges even.

2 Cut a 6½ x 2¼-inch piece of purple textured paper from Creative Pack; adhere to bottom of back flap, side and bottom edges even.

3 Using adhesive dots, adhere gingham-checked ribbon across bottom edge of front flap; trim edges even.

4 Position slide mount on the diagonal; adhere lavender words printed paper from Creative Pack to slide mount and trim edges even around inner opening and outer edges; ink edges black.

Materials
Cardmaker's 5 x 6½-inch blank white card
Cardmaker's Citrus Creative Pack (includes lavender words, pink/lavender polka-dot and purple textured printed papers and "Friendship" cutout)
Black-and-white circular slide mount
Black ink pad
Cardmaker's Citrus ribbons: 6½-inch piece ⅜-inch-wide dark pink-and-white gingham-checked, 5-inch piece ½-inch-wide dark pink sheer
Craft knife
Paper adhesive
Adhesive foam tape
Adhesive dots

5 Tie dark pink sheer ribbon around left corner of slide mount; knot ends on front.

6 Adhere "Friendship" cutout from Creative Pack to slide mount behind opening.

7 Using adhesive foam tape throughout, center and adhere slide mount to tea bag folded motif. Center tea bag folded motif on card as shown and adhere to top flap. ❀

Sources: Cardmaker's card, Creative Pack and ribbons from Hot Off The Press; slide mount from Slide Mount Mania.

Posy Pocket Greeting

DESIGN BY **JULIE EBERSOLE**

Tea Bag Folded Motif

1 Cut eight 1-inch squares from origami paper. Fold each square as follows:

2 Fold square in half on the diagonal, wrong sides facing; crease and unfold.

3 Position square right side down on the diagonal with crease running vertically. Referring to Figs. 1 and 2 for Celebrate, page 127, fold sides in to meet in center.

4 Punch or cut a 1½-inch circle from a scrap card stock or origami paper. Referring to photo throughout, arrange and adhere tea bag folded shapes edge to edge on circle to form a flower.

Assembly

1 Fold note card in half, right sides facing, forming a 3 x 5½-inch pocket with fold at bottom.

2 Referring to photo throughout, stamp Fancy Borders repeatedly on plain front of pocket.

FABULOUS FOLDS FOR CARD MAKING

Materials
Card stock: black, ivory
Red/white polka-dot note card
Printed origami paper
Black scalloped paper frills
1⅛-inch-diameter paper flower
Stamp sets: Fancy Borders #3-FANCSM, Circle Frame #2-CRFM
Black dye ink
White extra-fine point paint pen
1⅜-inch-diameter felt flower
Small black button
10 inches ¼-inch-wide black grosgrain ribbon with white stitches
Natural fine twine
Punches: ¼-inch hole, 1½-inch circle (optional), corner rounder, 1⅛ x 1⅝-inch tag
Paper adhesive

3 Trim ¾ inch off top edge of pocket front; turn cut end down to front another ¾ inch. Round off top corners on back portion of pocket.

4 Wrap ribbon around turned-down edge on pocket front, knotting ribbon ends near right edge.

5 Cut a 3½-inch strip of scalloped paper frills; tuck under flap on pocket front and adhere. Secure sides of pocket with staples.

6 Punch tag from black card stock; write sentiment on tag using white paint pen. Punch hole through end of tag; thread twine through hole and tie tag to ribbon on pocket near right edge.

7 Adhere folded motif to pocket front near left edge. Knot twine through button and clip ends on front; center and adhere button to paper flower, then to felt flower, then to folded motif.

8 *Note card:* Round off corners on a 4½ x 3-inch rectangle cut from ivory card stock. Stamp circles in corners; tuck note card into pocket. ✸

Sources: Note card, stamps and ribbon from A Muse Artstamps; Scalloped Paper Frills from Doodlebug Design Inc.; Elizabeth Blossoms & Buttons paper flower, felt flower and button from Making Memories; paint pen from Sharpie; punches from EK Sucess Ltd.

129

Happy Thoughts

DESIGN BY **JULIE EBERSOLE**

Project Note

Adhere elements using paper adhesive unless instructed otherwise.

Tea Bag Folded Butterfly Wings

1 Cut two 2-inch squares from polka-dot printed paper. Form each into a butterfly wing as follows:

2 Position paper square on the diagonal, printed side down. Fold square on the diagonal, wrong sides facing (Fig. 1).

3 With fold positioned at bottom, fold triangle in half (Fig. 2); unfold.

4 Fold top of triangle down (Fig. 3) so that top point extends somewhat below bottom edge (Fig. 4).

5 Fold sides down on the diagonal (Fig. 4). Resulting shape should look like butterfly wings (Fig. 5).

Assembly

1 Form a 5½ x 4¼-inch top-folded card from white card stock.

2 Referring to photo throughout, cut a 5¼ x 4-inch piece of blocks printed paper; center and adhere to card front.

3 Temporarily position butterfly wings on card to determine layout; remove. Punch dragonfly from black card stock; trim off wings, leaving only body. Adhere body to card for butterfly body. Draw antennae using fine-tip marker. Adhere folded wings using mini glue dots.

4 Dot flight path across card as shown using fine-tip marker. Stamp tiny butterflies on card using chalk inks.

5 Stamp "happy thoughts" onto diamonds printed paper using solvent-based ink; trim rectangle around words and adhere to card in lower right corner.

6 Thread floss through button; knot ends on front and trim. Adhere button to contrasting printed paper; trim edges even. Adhere button to upper right edge of stamped sentiment using mini glue dots. ✹

Sources: Rubber stamps from A Muse Artstamps; chalk inks from Clearsnap Inc.; solvent-based ink from Tsukineko Inc.; dragonfly punch from McGill Inc.

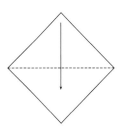

Fig. 1

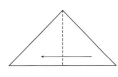

Fig. 2

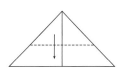

Fig. 3

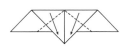

Fig. 4

Fig. 5

Sealed With a Kiss

DESIGN BY **MELANIE DOUTHIT**

Tea Bag Folded Butterfly Wings

1 Cut two 2-inch squares of Sweetheart printed paper.

2 Referring to drawings for Happy Thoughts, page 131, fold each square into a butterfly wing with turquoise side showing.

Assembly

1 Form a 6½ x 4-inch top-folded card from light blue card stock.

2 Referring to photo throughout, cut a 6⁵⁄₁₆ x 3¹¹⁄₁₆-inch piece from pink grid side of Nothing to Lose Printed paper; center and adhere to card front. Cut a 5¾ x 3¼-inch piece from brown/multicolored side of Air Mail printed paper; center and adhere to card front.

3 Cut a 6⁵⁄₁₆ x ¾-inch strip from XOX side of Nothing to Lose printed paper; adhere to card front ⅞ inch from bottom.

4 Trim "Love ya!" and "SWAK" images from Air Mail printed paper; ink edges of "SWAK" image. Adhere images to card as shown.

5 Adhere butterfly wings to right side of card as shown. Use paper piercer to make stitching holes for butterfly's body and antennae in card front; stitch with embroidery floss, securing floss ends on reverse side. ✸

Source: Hugs-n-Kisses printed paper from Dream Street Papers.

Materials

Light blue card stock
Printed paper: Sweetheart, Nothing to Lose, Air Mail
Reddish brown ink
Pink embroidery floss
Embroidery needle
Paper piercer
Paper adhesive

Asian Butterfly

DESIGN BY **JULIE EBERSOLE**

Tea Bag Folded Butterfly

1 Cut two 2-inch squares from origami paper.

2 Referring to diagrams and instructions for making Tea Bag Folded Butterfly for Happy Thoughts, page 131, fold each square into a butterfly wing.

Assembly

1 Form a 4¼-inch-square top-folded card from light green card stock.

2 Cut a 3⅞-inch square from dark blue card stock; center and cut 2⅜-inch circle in card stock using circle-cutting system. Referring to photo throughout, stamp white dots around opening.

3 Adhere origami paper to dark blue card stock behind opening.

Materials

Card stock: light green, dark blue, cream
Origami paper
Dotted Circle stamp #2-CRFM from Circle Frames Stamp Set
White pigment ink
Extra-fine white paint pen
10 inches ³⁄₁₆-inch-wide pale green piping-edged sheer organdy ribbon
2 cream eyelets
Punches: ⅛-inch hole, 1-inch butterfly
Eyelet-setting tool
Circle-cutting system with 2⅜-inch circle die
Paper adhesive

4 Punch ⅛-inch holes in upper corners of dark blue card stock; set eyelets in holes. Thread ribbon through eyelets; knot ends on front near left edge; trim.

5 Center and adhere dark blue card stock to card front.

6 Punch butterfly from cream card stock; adhere to card front over lower right edge of circular cutout.

7 Adhere folded butterfly wings to card over wings of punched card-stock butterfly. Add antennae using paint pen. ✱

Sources: Stamp and ribbon from A Muse Artstamps; Coluzzle circle-cutting system from Provo Craft; Martha Stewart punch from EK Success Ltd.; paint pen from Sharpie.

133

Sparkling Rain Card

DESIGN BY **DONNA MALIGNO**

Tea Bag Folded Umbrella

1 *Make fiber sheet:* Place a clump of white fibers on sheet of parchment paper, using enough to make a sheet approximately 5½ inches square when pressed flat. Cover fibers with a second parchment sheet. Using iron set on medium or polyester setting, press firmly for 3–10 seconds. Peel off parchment; let cool.

2 Punch four scalloped ovals from fiber sheet. Fold each piece as follows:

3 Fold oval in half with fold perpendicular to its shorter dimension. Referring to Fig. 1, fold down one side until folded edge touches center. Repeat with other side (Fig. 2). Press creases firmly.

4 With seams facing down, arrange folded ovals so that they overlap, with folded edge of one shape aligning with center line of adjacent shape (Fig. 3). Continue until all pieces are arranged in an umbrella shape.

5 Open end folds on end pieces (Fig. 4). Adhere remaining sections together where they overlap.

6 Flip umbrella wrong side up; adhere B to B and A to A (Fig. 5). Fold A panels over adjacent edge of umbrella and adhere; repeat with B panels on opposite edge.

Assembly

1 Form a 4¼ x 5½-inch side-folded card from yellow card stock.

2 Cut a 4¼ x 5½-inch piece from white card stock; trim edges with paper cutter and scallop blade; center and adhere to card front.

3 Cut a 3⅝ x 1½-inch strip from yellow card stock; trim long edges with paper cutter and scallop blade. Cut a 3⅝ x ¹¹⁄₁₆-inch strip from white card stock; center and adhere to yellow strip.

4 Referring to photo throughout, wrap sheer pink polka-dot ribbon around card-stock strips; knot ends on front and trim. Tie sheer yellow ribbon around pink knot; knot ends and trim.

5 Cut a 3⅝ x 4¾-inch piece from pink card stock. Adhere card-stock strips with ribbons to pink card stock ⅜ inch from bottom. Center and adhere pink card stock to card front.

6 Cut 2-inch umbrella handle from scrap of fiber sheet; coat with glitter glue and let dry. Adhere to card front.

7 Adhere umbrella to card front at top of handle; apply glitter glue along scalloped edges. Tie white ribbon in a tiny bow; adhere to base of handle.

8 Dot scallops on white card stock using pink brush-tip marker. Dot scallops on yellow card stock using white pigment pen.

9 Add "raindrops" of gloss medium to pink card-stock background as desired; sprinkle with glitter. ✽

Sources: Fantasy Fibers from Art Institute Glitter; Inkssentials pigment pen, Stickles glitter glue and Glossy Accents gloss medium from Ranger Industries Inc.; Brushables brush-tip marker from EK Success Ltd.; paper cutter and punch from Marvy Uchida.

Materials

Card stock: white, yellow, pink
White acrylic fibers
Pink brush-tip marker
White pigment pen
Gloss medium
Iridescent glitter glue
White glitter
Ribbon: 12 inches ½-inch-wide sheer pink polka-dot, 5 inches ⅜-inch-wide sheer yellow, 4 inches ⅛-inch-wide white satin
Nonstick iron and ironing board
Parchment paper
Paper cutter with Scallop blade
Mega Oval Scallop punch
Permanent tape

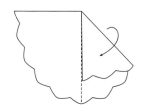

Fig. 1

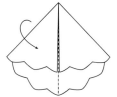

Fig. 2

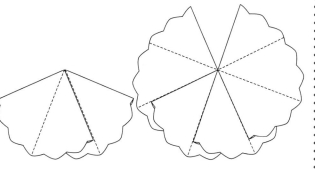

Fig. 3   **Fig. 4**

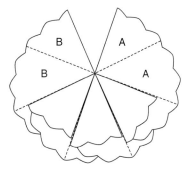

Fig. 5

Patriotic Celebration

DESIGN BY **SUSAN HUBER**

FABULOUS FOLDS FOR CARD MAKING

Tea Bag Folded Star

1 Cut seven 2-inch squares from star printed paper. Position squares on the diagonal, printed side down. Fold each square as follows:

2 Fold square in half diagonally from top to bottom. Unfold, then fold sides in so that outer edges meet along the center line (Fig. 1).

3 Folded shape should look like Fig. 2.

4 Fold top right edge down (Fig. 3) so that corner A meets left side (Fig. 4).

5 Unfold previous fold (Fig. 5).

6 Fold top left edge down so that corner A meets right side (Fig. 6); unfold.

7 Shape should look like Fig. 7.

8 Take point C; pinching the fold between your thumb and finger, pull it out and down to the left, creasing along the fold line made in the step accompanying Fig. 6 (Fig. 8).

9 Paper looks like Fig. 9 while being folded.

10 Folded shape should look like Fig. 10.

11 Fold point A by pulling it up and over to left side so that side point meets center fold (Fig. 11).

12 Folded shape should look like Fig. 12.

13 Fold point A to the right, creasing along center fold line (Fig. 13).

14 Folded shape should look like Fig. 14.

15 Separate layers of the triangle (point A). Grasp point A and pull it down to center line (Fig. 15); flatten the paper to form a diamond shape.

16 Folded shape should look like Fig. 16.

17 Turn shape over so other side is facing you (Fig. 17).

18 Apply a small amount of adhesive to back of triangle C. Slip the right side of the first piece between the short leg and diamond shape on back of second piece (Fig. 18).

19 One by one, attach remaining pieces in this manner until star is complete (Fig. 19).

Materials

Blue textured card stock
Printed paper: weathered flag, red/white star print
"Celebrate!" rubber stamp
Blue ink pad
Blue star brad
Punches: ⅟₁₆-inch hole, 1-inch circle
Double-sided tape
Paper adhesive
Adhesive foam tape

Assembly

Project Note

Adhere elements using paper adhesive unless instructed otherwise.

1 Form a 6¼ x 4-inch top-folded card from blue card stock.

2 Cut a 6 x 3¼-inch piece of flag printed paper; adhere to card front ⅛ inch from fold.

3 Punch a 1-inch circle from star printed paper; center and adhere to folded star. Punch a ¹⁄₁₆-inch hole through center of star; attach brad.

Referring to photo throughout, adhere star to upper left corner of card as shown.

4 Stamp "Celebrate!" on white stripe of another piece of flag printed paper. Trim rectangle around word; adhere to card stock and trim, leaving very narrow borders.

5 Adhere stamped image to bottom right corner of card ½ inch from right edge and ¼ inch from bottom using adhesive foam tape. ❋

Sources: Printed paper from Rusty Pickle; stamp from Stampin' Up!; brad from Queen & Co.

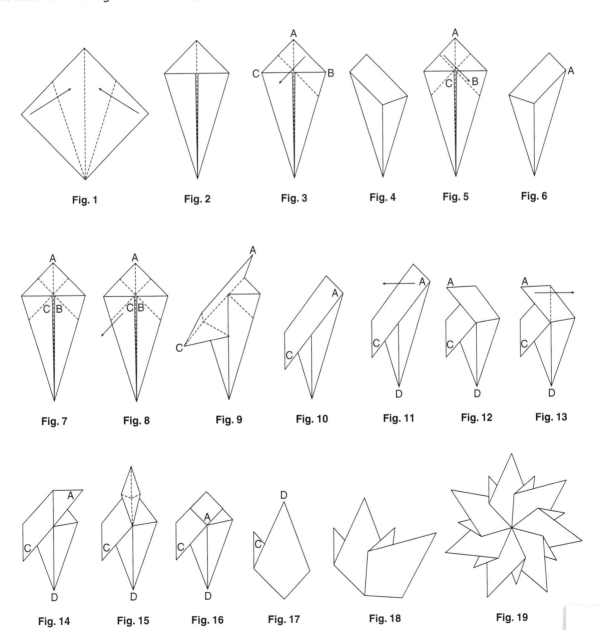

Fig. 1 **Fig. 2** **Fig. 3** **Fig. 4** **Fig. 5** **Fig. 6**

Fig. 7 **Fig. 8** **Fig. 9** **Fig. 10** **Fig. 11** **Fig. 12** **Fig. 13**

Fig. 14 **Fig. 15** **Fig. 16** **Fig. 17** **Fig. 18** **Fig. 19**

POP-UPS

Young and old alike will love receiving these pop-up greeting cards. Perfect for nearly any occasion, learn how pop-ups add a fun surprise to quick-and-easy designs. With a few simple folds of card stock and a little bit of imagination, you'll be creating original cards like these in no time.

It's hard to decide which is more fun: making a pop-up card or receiving one. Get your friends and family in on the act, and you can have it both ways.

Pop-up cards do what the name says they do: they pop up when you open them.

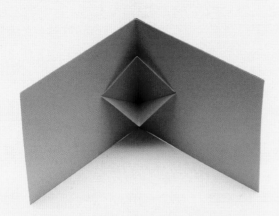

This simple angle or bird's beak pop-up is quick and easy to create with only a craft knife and a scoring tool.

The simplest pop-ups require only one or two cut lines, folded inward to create a small block or wedge. With more cuts, it's easy to create stair steps and other more complex pop-ups with multiple levels.

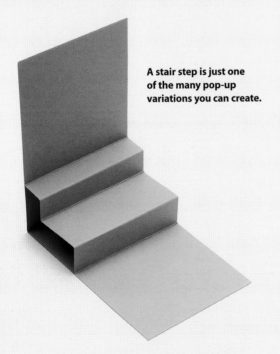

A stair step is just one of the many pop-up variations you can create.

Pop-up elements can be shaped like letters, trees, animals and more. You can glue all sorts of things to the cut and folded areas, too. Inside the card is a miniature theater that can be whatever you want it to be.

The exterior of a pop-up card is attached after

This die cut from Sizzix provides a quick short cut to creating pop-up cards.

the cutting and inside assembly is completed, like putting a jacket on over a party dress—a finishing touch that is important to the construction of the card as well as to the look of it. Without that extra layer, the outside of a card would reveal all the holes and wouldn't stand firmly, as it should.

Pop-up cards can fold across the top or at the side. Any time you have at least one fold and two panels, you have room for a pop-up inside—which means that you can create multiple pop-ups inside accordion-fold cards and two pop-ups inside gatefold and fold-back cards.

Things to Remember, Supplies You'll Need

Pop-up cards require stiff, sturdy card stock, plus careful scoring, cutting and folding.

If you use a template, make sure to follow the manufacturer's directions. For some templates, trace the design on the back of the card stock before cutting; for others (metal), cut while the template is taped in position.

Keep a roll of temporary, removable/reusable tape handy; you'll need it regardless of what kind of template you use.

Make sure your craft knife has the right blade and that the blade is sharp. Practice on scraps of card stock to make sure you know how much hand pressure you need.

A few words about safety worth repeating—always keep sharp tools away from children and pets. Pay attention as you cut; you only have one pair of hands. ✳

Deck the Halls

DESIGN BY **JULIA STAINTON**

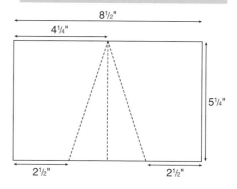

Deck the Halls

1 Form a 4¼ x 5½-inch side-folded card from card stock.

2 Cut a 4 x 5¼-inch piece of Season of Joy printed paper; center and adhere to card front.

3 Referring to photo throughout, cut Deck the Halls sentiment from printed paper; adhere to card front near lower left corner. Attach felt snowflake over lower right corner of sentiment using photo mount.

4 *Pop-up:* Cut an 8½ x 5¼-inch piece from green side of Fruitcake printed paper; fold according to diagram, creasing well.

5 Open folded paper, folding center triangular tree section outward. Randomly attach red eyelets in triangular tree for "decorations."

6 Apply adhesive to reverse side of printed paper outside tree area; adhere paper inside of card, making sure tree is folded so that it will pop out when card is opened.

7 Embellish inside of card with strips of Naughty and Nice printed paper; apply rub-on sentiments desired. Tie ribbon in knot; adhere to design. ❋

Sources: Season of Joy printed papers from Scrapworks; ribbon, Felt Heritage snowflake and photo turn from Creative Impressions; Crop-A-Dile II Big Bite eyelet set from We R Memory Keepers.

Posy Pop-up

DESIGN BY **JULIE EBERSOLE**

Materials

Card stock: white, light green, pink
3½ x 5-inch chiffon yellow note card
Polka-dot printed papers: pink, grass
Stamps: Tiny Bee, "hi, friend," "friends
  make life blossom," Stitched Pinwheel
  Background, Fancy Borders
Ink: lime chalk, dark pink chalk, black
Yellow sparkle marker
Giga Flower Punch
Craft knife
Paper adhesive

friends make life blossom

1 Cut a 2 x 2½-inch piece of white card stock.
Referring to photo throughout, stamp
lime quilted background onto card stock;
add stamped solid ribbon border for flower stem.

2 Adhere stamped card stock to light green
card stock; cut out, leaving ⅛-inch light green
borders. Center and adhere card-stock panel to
card ⅞ inch from top.

3 Stamp "friends make life blossom" in black
onto card front just below stamped panel.

4 Punch Giga flower from pink card stock;
adhere to card front at top of stem. Cut a leaf
shape from grass polka-dot printed paper; adhere
to card front as shown.

5 Punch Giga flower from pink polka-dot printed
paper; ink edges pink. Score petals where
indicated by dashed lines on diagram.

6 Stamp plain side of flower sentiment and bee
using black ink; color bee with sparkle marker.

7 Crease flower along scored lines and compress
to close. Center and adhere closed flower to
pink card-stock flower on card. ❁

Sources: Note card, printed paper and stamps from A Muse
Artstamps; chalk inks from Clearsnap Inc.; Spica Twinkle marker by
Copic; flower punch from Marvy Uchida.

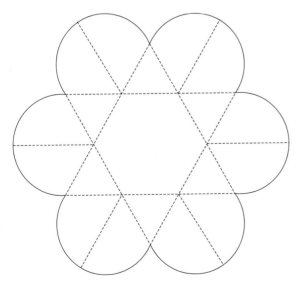

Hi, Friend Posy Pop-up

Enjoy

DESIGN BY **LINDA BEESON**

Project Note

Ink all edges of printed paper and chipboard shapes.

1 Cut a 5½ x 8½-inch piece each from Lively Scroll and Picture Perfect printed papers. Fold Lively Scroll paper in half wrong sides facing to form exterior of a 5½ x 4¼-inch top-folded card; fold Picture Perfect printed paper in half right sides facing to form card interior.

2 Pop-up tabs: With Picture Perfect card interior closed, use craft knife to make cuts through fold and perpendicular to it, referring to diagram for placement. Open card interior and fold closed again, pushing pop-up tabs to inside.

3 Referring to photo throughout, attach flowers and leaves to fronts of outside pop-up tabs with mini brads.

Materials

Printed paper: Lively Scroll, Picture Perfect, Birds Nest, Green Lace
Chipboard embellishments: ⅝-inch "enjoy," 2¼ x 2⅝-inch house
Antique tan chalk ink pad
Black alphabet rub-on transfers
Glitter Bird sticker
3 old gold mini brads
Felt flowers: 1¼-inch black, ¾-inch red, ¾-inch white
2 pairs felt leaves
Craft knife and cutting mat
Paper adhesive

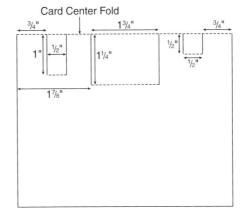

Enjoy Card

4 Adhere Green Lace printed paper to chipboard house roof; adhere Birds Nest printed paper to house. Trim all edges even. Adhere Green Lace paper behind openings in house; adhere house to front of center pop-up tab.

5 Adhere Glitter Bird to upper right corner of card interior. Apply rub-on transfers to spell "new home" near bottom.

6 Adhere card layers, avoiding pop-up tabs and trimming edges of interior as needed.

7 Adhere chipboard "enjoy" to card front in lower right corner. Poke mini brad through small white flower; adhere flower to card front as shown. ✳

Sources: Lively Scroll and 1000 Words printed papers from My Mind's Eye; Spring Fling Green Lace and Birds Nest printed papers from Pink Paislee; chipboard house from Maya Road; rub-on transfers and chipboard "enjoy" from Making Memories; Glitter Bird sticker from K&Company; felt flowers and leaves from Creative Impressions.

Forever Friend

DESIGN BY **KELLY ANNE GRUNDHAUSER**

Materials

Printed paper: white/aqua pin-dot, orange, turquoise, light green
Die-cuts: sister-themed sentiments, branch, four flowers, small bird
Tiny black flower border rub-on transfer
Distressing tool
Instant-dry paper adhesive

1 Form a 5¼ x 5½-inch top-folded card from pin-dot printed paper.

2 Cut a 5⅛ x 2-inch strip of turquoise printed paper, a 5 x 1½-inch strip of orange printed paper, and a 4⅞ x ½-inch strip from light green printed paper; distress edges of all paper pieces.

3 Referring to photo throughout, adhere turquoise strip to card front ½ inch from bottom. Adhere orange paper strip to turquoise paper and light green strip to orange strip; they need not be centered.

4 Apply tiny flower border rub-on transfer to light green paper strip as shown.

5 Adhere sister-themed die cut over layered printed-paper strips slightly to right of center.

6 Cut 1- to 1½-inch x ¼-inch-wide strip from card stock; fold strip accordion-style to form a "spring." Adhere flower to one end of "spring"; adhere other end of spring to upper left corner of sister-themed die cut.

7 *Inside card:* Adhere branch die cut and sentiment. Cut "spring" four more times from card stock; adhere to three flowers and small bird die cut; adhere to card. ✻

Sources: Printed paper, die cuts and rub-on transfer from Crate Paper; distressing tool from Ranger Industries; Zip-Dry Paper Glue from Beacon Adhesives Inc.

Dreams Come True

DESIGN BY **KATHLEEN PANEITZ**

Materials

Card stock: white, fuchsia
Printed paper: Bubblegum,
   Green Gingham
Pink scalloped note cards: round, oval
Embossed glitter stickers: "Dreams come
   true," "princess"
Dimensional stickers: flowers, princess
Rosey alphabet stickers
⅜-inch-wide pink/lavender
   polka-dot ribbon
Paper adhesive

1 Form a 5½ x 4¼-inch top-folded card from white card stock.

2 *Pop-up tab:* With card closed, use craft knife to make cuts through fold and perpendicular to it, referring to diagram for placement. Open card interior and fold closed again, pushing pop-up tab to inside.

3 Adhere Green Gingham printed paper to card front, avoiding pop-up tab; trim edges even.

4 Cut a 5½ x 2-inch strip of Bubblegum printed paper; center and adhere to card front.

5 Center and adhere round scalloped note card to card front. Adhere "dreams come true" sticker to fuchsia card stock; cut out, leaving ⅛-inch fuchsia borders.

6 Adhere dimensional flower stickers to card front; add bow tied from ribbon.

Card Interior

1 Cut 1 inch off bottom of oval scalloped note card. Adhere larger portion to pop-up strip, leaving a little space at bottom so that card will open and close smoothly. Adhere cut-off portion to bottom inside of card adjacent to rest of oval.

2 Adhere dimensional princess sticker to scalloped oval on pop-up. Adhere alphabet stickers to spell "sweet" and princess glitter sticker to bottom inside of card. ✶

Sources: Printed paper from Crate Paper (Bubblegum) and Making Memories (Green Gingham); scalloped note cards from Jenni Bowlin; Princess Icons embossed glitter and dimensional stickers from K&Company; alphabet stickers from Chatterbox; ribbon from Heidi Grace Designs.

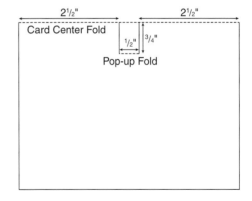

Dreams Come True

Just Me

DESIGN BY **KATHLEEN PANEITZ**

1 Form a 6-inch-square side-folded card from white card stock.

2 *Pop-up tab:* With card closed, use craft knife to make cuts through fold and perpendicular to it, referring to diagram for placement. Open card interior and fold closed again, pushing pop-up tab to inside.

3 Adhere flowers portion of printed paper to top half of card front, avoiding pop-up

Materials

Card stock: white, terra-cotta
Euphoria printed paper
"Just Me" Jotter journaling card
Chipboard flower
Garden Party green printed blossoms
Sunrise Smoothie card-stock stickers: oval, flowers
Rub-on transfers
Sunrise Smoothie epoxy brads
Tiny Daisy 5/16-inch-wide orange ribbon with white flowers
Yellow floss
Wooden craft sticks

tab; adhere yellow portion of printed paper to bottom half of card front. Trim edges even.

4 Center and adhere "Just Me" journaling card to card front; embellish with stickers and ribbon bow.

Card Interior

1 Fold a piece of terra-cotta card stock in half. Position flower pot pattern along fold and cut out. Score flower pot horizontally $7/8$ inch from top; fold down for flower pot rim. Adhere flower pot to pop-up tab.

2 Adhere printed paper to chipboard flower; trim edges even. Attach epoxy brads to centers of chipboard flower and green blossom flowers.

3 Adhere flowers to craft-stick "stems." Adhere sticks inside flower pot as shown. Adhere a bow of yellow floss to flower pot.

4 Add sentiments using rub-on transfers. ✺

Sources: Printed paper from We R Memory Keepers; Random Musings Jotter and "Cheer up" rub-on transfer from Luxe Designs; chipboard flower from Li'l Davis Designs; Garden Party green printed blossoms from Making Memories; Sunrise Smoothie card-stock stickers and epoxy brads from Cloud 9 Design; rub-on transfer from 7gypsies; Adorn It ribbon from Carolee's Creations.

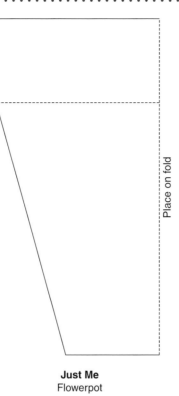

Place on fold

Just Me
Flowerpot

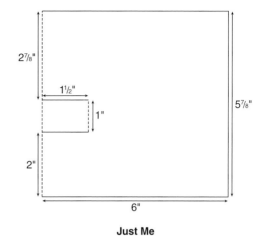

2⅞"   1½"   1"   5⅞"

2"   6"

Just Me

Me & You Pop-up Card

DESIGN BY **SUE ELDRED**

Materials
Card stock: turquoise, very dark
    turquoise, green
Classic K Margo printed paper pad
Classic K Margo Adhesive Chipboard
    words, buttons, butterflies, flowers
Classic K Margo Ornament and Words
    rub-on transfers
10 inches silver craft wire
Wire cutters
Craft knife and cutting mat
Double-sided tape
Clear packing tape

Card Exterior

Form a 6-inch-square top-folded card from turquoise card stock.

Card Front

1 Cut a 5½-inch square of very dark turquoise card stock and a 5¼-inch square of burgundy printed paper; center and adhere burgundy paper to very dark turquoise paper.

2 Cut a 5¼ x 2¾-inch piece of turquoise printed paper; adhere to burgundy printed paper cut in step 1 with side and bottom edges even. Center and adhere card-stock/printed-paper panel to card front.

3 Referring to photo throughout, apply turquoise border rub-on transfer over seam between burgundy and turquoise printed papers on card front.

4 Adhere chipboard "me & you" to card front. Adhere small chipboard flowers to words; adhere "Precious" to lower right corner.

Card Interior

1 Cut a 5¼ x 11½-inch piece of floral printed paper; fold in half, right sides facing, to form background of card interior.

2 Cut a 5½ x 5¾-inch piece of turquoise printed paper; adhere to right side of floral printed paper with top and side edges even. Fold card interior closed.

3 Pop-up tab: With card interior closed, use craft knife to make cuts through fold and perpendicular to it, referring to diagram for placement. Open card interior and fold closed again, pushing pop-up tab to inside.

4 Adhere double-sided tape to top half of card interior; avoiding pop-up tab; insert into card and adhere. Adhere double-sided tape to bottom half of card interior; press onto card.

5 Carefully peel away the adhesive layer on back of chipboard butterfly and "my life with you is complete" stickers. Using clear packing tape, affix one end of a 5-inch piece of wire to reverse side of each butterfly; bend wires to give butterflies movement. Using clear packing tape, affix the wires to the reverse side of the "my life is complete" sticker.

6 Reinforcement for pop-up tab: Cut a 1½ x 3½-inch piece of turquoise printed paper. Score strip horizontally ½ inch, 1¼ inches, 2 inches and 2¾ inches from top edge. Fold scored strip into an open-ended block, adhering overlapping ends. Adhere reinforcement inside card on top of pop-up tab so that it will collapse along scored lines, flattening completely when card is closed.

7 Adhere double-sided adhesive to front of pop-up tab and reinforcing block; adhere "My Life is Complete" chipboard sticker to pop-ups.

8 Cut 5¼ x 2-inch strip of green gingham printed paper; adhere near bottom of floral printed paper inside card. Adhere green floral border rub-on transfer to seam between printed papers.

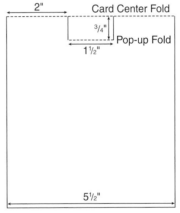

Me & You Pop-up

9 Cut a 2-inch square from burgundy printed paper; cut in half on the diagonal. Adhere triangles to corners of floral printed paper at fold, edges even.

10 Apply "you are the one" rub-on transfer to tan printed paper; trim around words. Adhere tan paper to green card stock and trim, leaving ⅛-inch borders. Center and adhere to card as shown.

11 Embellish card as desired with additional rub-on transfers and chipboard stickers. ✻

Source: Printed paper pad, chipboard words, stickers and rub-on transfer from K&Company.

Bright Side of Life

DESIGN BY **LINDSEY BOTKIN**

Project Note

Adhere elements using paper adhesive unless instructed otherwise.

Form a 4¼-inch square top-fold card from black card stock.

Card Interior

1 Cut a 7¾ x 4-inch piece of white card stock and a 7½ x 3¾-inch piece of Playful printed paper; center and adhere printed paper to white card stock. Fold in half, printed paper sides facing.

2 Pop-up tab: With card interior closed, use craft knife to make cuts through fold and perpendicular to it, referring to diagram for placement. Open card interior and fold closed again, pushing pop-up tab to inside.

3 Referring to photo throughout, stamp five butterflies onto white card stock; when dry, use markers to color butterflies in colors that complement printed paper. Cut out.

Materials

Card stock: black, white
Printed paper: Playful, Wicked Fun
Fluttering By stamp set
Black solvent-based ink
Black/transparent decorative adhesive tape
8 inches ½-inch-wide sheer white polka-dot ribbon
Markers, including fine-tip black
Punches: 2-inch circle, 2½-inch scalloped circle
Paper piercer
Craft knife and cutting mat
Paper adhesive
Glue dots

4 Build an arrangement of three butterflies on a scrap square of white card stock, adhering butterflies to card-stock base and to each other at different levels using glue dots. Adhere background square to front of pop-up tab.

5 Adhere fourth butterfly to upper left corner of card interior; reserve fifth butterfly for card front.

FABULOUS FOLDS FOR CARD MAKING

150

Card Front

1 Cut a 4-inch square of Wicked Fun printed paper. Use paper piercer to pierce evenly spaced holes across top ³⁄₁₆ inch from edge; join holes with faux "stitches" using fine-tip black marker.

2 Adhere a strip of decorative tape across bottom of printed paper ⅝ inch from edge. Center and adhere printed paper square to card front.

3 Cut a 4 x 1¾-inch strip from Playful printed paper. Wrap ribbon around strip near left edge and knot ends on front; trim. Adhere printed paper to card front 1 inch from bottom.

4 Punch scalloped circle from black card stock and circle from white card stock; center and adhere white circle to black scalloped circle. Center and adhere remaining butterfly to circle using glue dot; adhere circles with butterfly to card front over printed-paper strip, ¼ inch from right edge. ✹

Sources: Dude Line printed papers and Clearly IOD Tape from Prima Marketing; stamps from Verve Visual; solvent-based ink from Tsukineko; punches from Marvy Uchida.

3¾"

1"

⅞"

Card Center Fold

Bright Side of Life

Always look on the bright side of life.

Girlfriends

DESIGN BY **MELONY BRADLEY**

Card Pocket

1 Cut a 6-inch square each from pink and light green card stock; round corners with corner rounder punch; ink edges with chalk ink. Pink will be front of card pocket; light green will be back.

2 Using watermark ink and butterfly stamp, stamp pink card stock randomly, stamping some images off edges. Using black pigment ink, stamp one butterfly on a scrap of light green card stock; cut out and reserve.

3 Referring to diagram, use craft knife to cut flap in pink card stock.

4 Butterfly panel: Cut a 2½ x 3½-inch piece and a 2 x 3-inch piece from printed paper; cut a 2¼ x 3⅛-inch piece from light green card stock. Ink edges with chalk ink. Center and adhere smaller printed-paper piece to green card stock, and card stock to larger piece of printed paper. Adhere stamped light green butterfly to layered panel as shown; embellish with self-adhesive rhinestone. Center and adhere bottom edge of panel to pocket front so that top edge of panel is ⅝ inch from top.

5 Punch flowers from light green card stock; adhere to pocket front as desired and embellish with self-adhesive rhinestones.

Tag

1 Cut a 3 x 5-inch piece from light green card stock; round off corners using corner rounder punch. Ink edges with chalk ink.

2 Stamp sentiments at top and bottom edges of tag. Center and punch a ⅛-inch hole near top edge; thread ribbon through hole and knot.

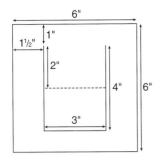

Girlfriends

Assembly

1 Hold pocket front and back together, wrong sides facing. Center and punch half of a 1-inch circle through both layers at top edge.

2 Insert tag into pocket so that it protrudes ½–¾ inch from top. Gently lift flap in pocket front; apply adhesive to bottom edge of flap and press down onto underlying surface of tag. (Tag will be adhered to flap above stamped sentiment at bottom of tag.)

3 Adhere pocket front to back along edges of sides and bottom only; let dry.

4 To "open card," gently pull tag from top of pocket, exposing sentiment at top of tag; flap will be pulled up to expose stamped sentiment at bottom of tag. ✷

Sources: Printed paper from The Paper Studio; stamps from Autumn Leaves (butterfly), Rubber Stampede ("Friends Today") and Hampton Art Stamps ("Girlfriendship"); Zip Dry Paper Glue from Beacon Adhesives Inc.

Materials

Card stock: pink, light green
Enchanted Leaves printed paper
Stamps: butterfly, "Friends today," "Girlfriendship"
Ink: watermark, black pigment, black chalk
Self-adhesive pink rhinestones
6 inches ⅜-inch-wide black grosgrain ribbon with white stitches
Punches: corner rounder, ⅛-inch hole, 1-inch circle, 1-inch flower
Craft knife and cutting mat
Instant-dry paper glue

My Hero

DESIGN BY **LAURA NICHOLAS,** COURTESY OF HOT OFF THE PRESS

1. Cut a 5-inch square of black card stock; adhere to card front.

2. Referring to photo throughout, cut a 4⅝ x 4½-inch piece of color block printed paper with a 1⅞-inch-high block of red at the top; ink edges.

3. Wrap ribbon around printed paper over striped section; adhere ends on back. Center and adhere printed paper to card front. Knot a short piece of ribbon; trim ends at an angle and adhere knot to ribbon on card to right of center.

4. Lightly sand helmet and fire hydrant Brad Buddies; attach to yellow and blue blocks on card front with brads according to manufacturer's instructions.

5. Hand-print, or use a computer to generate, hero definition onto white card stock to fit within an area measuring approximately 3½ x 1 inch; cut out and ink edges. Adhere to black card stock and cut out, leaving narrow borders. Center and adhere definition to red block using adhesive foam tape.

Card Interior

1. *Pop-up block:* Cut a 2 x 3½-inch piece of black card stock. Score strip horizontally ½ inch, 1¼ inches, 2 inches and 2¾ inches from top edge. Fold scored strip into an open-ended block, adhering overlapping ends. Using glue dots and referring to Fig. 1, adhere pop-up block inside card against fold so that block will collapse along scored lines, flattening completely, when card is closed.

2. Trim a 3⅛ x 1¼-inch strip of color block printed paper with striped border along right edge of a 2⅝-inch-wide yellow block. Wrap ribbon around striped border as shown; adhere to reverse side.

Hero (n.) a legendary figure of great strength or ability, a man admired for his qualities and achievements, the chief male character in a dramatic work.

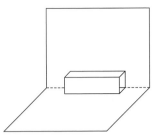

Fig. 1

Adhere printed paper to black card stock and trim, leaving narrow borders.

3 Lightly sand fire engine Brad Buddy and attach to yellow block using brads according to manufacturer's instructions. Adhere to front of pop-up block, leaving a little space at bottom so card will open and close smoothly.

4 Cut a 5 x 1½-inch strip of red textured paper; ink edges. Adhere across bottom inside of card, side and bottom edges even.

5 Hand-print, or use computer to generate, "You are our Hero!" onto white card stock; cut out. Adhere to black card stock and cut out, leaving narrow borders. Center and adhere to red card stock inside card. ✳

Sources: Printed paper and ribbon from Hot Off The Press; Brad Buddies from Paper Wishes.

Happy Birthday Flower Card

DESIGN BY **ALICIA THELIN,** COURTESY OF STAMPIN' UP!

Project Note

Adhere elements using paper adhesive unless instructed otherwise.

1 Form card from turquoise textured card stock; adhere ribbon to card as shown.

2 Adhere printed paper to card front and to chipboard number; trim edges even. Sand number lightly; adhere to card front.

Card Interior

1 Adhere printed paper inside top flap of card; trim edges even.

2 *Flower:* Cut stem from green textured card stock. Punch two flowers from printed paper; center end of stem between flowers and adhere. Punch another flower from orange textured card stock; adhere to printed paper flower using Stampin' Dimensionals. Punch a ½-inch circle from printed paper; adhere to center of flower.

3 *Pop-up:* Referring to Fig. 1, fold a ½-inch-wide strip of turquoise card stock into a stairstep "hinge." With card open at a 90-degree angle, adhere bottom tab A inside bottom of card; adhere top tab B to inside top of card. Adhere flower to front of hinge as shown.

4 Fold two ½-inch-wide strips of turquoise card stock into "bridge" hinges as shown in Fig. 2. Position hinges at outer edges of card next to fold. With card open at a 90-degree angle, adhere bottom tab A to inside bottom of card; adhere top tab to inside top of card.

5 Cut green textured card stock same size as bottom panel inside card; trim back long edge with scallop-edge punch. Adhere card stock to inner card bottom, side and front edges even; at back, fold up scalloped edge and adhere it to hinge fronts C.

6 Stamp "Happy Birthday" in orange and turquoise onto white card stock; trim and adhere to card. Embellish with strip of printed paper. ✱

Source: Printed paper, stamp set, Stampin' Dimensionals and punches from Stampin' Up!

Materials

Card stock: white, green textured, orange textured, turquoise textured
Rainbow Sherbet printed paper
Chipboard number
On Board Simon Upper
Happy Everything stamp set
Ink pads: orange, turquoise
¼-inch-wide orange grosgrain ribbon
Sandpaper
Punches: 5-Petal Flower, Scallop Edge, ½-inch circle
Stampin' Dimensionals
Paper adhesive

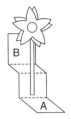

Fig. 1   Fig. 2

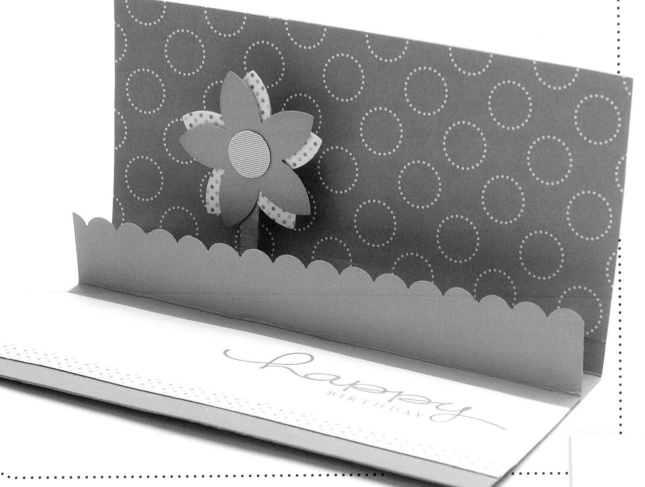

Gift Card Pop-up

DESIGN BY **MELONY BRADLEY**

Card Exterior

Form a 6½ x 5-inch top-folded card from dark beige card stock.

Card Interior

1 Cut a 6½ x 5-inch piece of printed paper; score horizontally 1 inch from top. Fold down top flap with right sides facing; referring to photos throughout, adhere larger portion of printed paper to interior of card with side and bottom edges even.

2 *Pop-up blocks:* Cut two strips from dark beige card stock each 1 x 4 inches. Beginning from top, score horizontally across each strip every ⅞ inch, scoring each strip four times (Fig. 1); fold into an open square (Fig. 2), and adhere at overlap. Position pop-up blocks on fold of card (Fig. 3), behind the 1-inch flap of printed paper standing up near fold of card; adhere pop-up blocks to sides of card and adhere printed-paper flap to front of pop-up blocks.

3 Cut a 5 x 3-inch piece of dark beige card stock; use alphabet stamps and black pigment ink to stamp "Enjoy" onto card stock. Center and adhere card stock inside card.

4 Apply flower rub-on transfers to inside card as desired.

Card Front

1 Cut a 6½ x 1¾-inch strip of printed paper; adhere to card 1¼ inches from top. Apply flower border rub-on transfers to card above and below printed-paper strip.

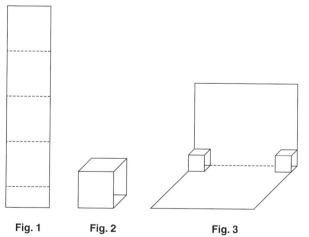

Fig. 1   Fig. 2   Fig. 3

2 Punch a 2-inch circle from dark beige card stock; embellish with stamped "for you" sentiment and flower rub-on transfer. Punch a 3-inch scalloped circle from black card stock. Center and adhere dark beige circle to black circle; center over printed paper strip and adhere to card ⅝ inch from right edge.

3 Attach black silk flower to ivory silk flower using pearl brad. Cut two 3-inch pieces of ribbon; trim ends at an angle. Adhere flower and ribbons to card front as shown.

4 Embellish card front with flower rub-on transfers as desired.

Use glue dot to secure a gift card inside card, between pop-up blocks and behind stand-up edge of printed paper. ✸

Sources: Printed paper from SEI; stamps from Plaid/All Night Studio; rub-on transfers from BasicGrey (Gypsy flowers) and Doodlebug Design Inc. (flower border); Zip Dry Paper Glue from Beacon Adhesives Inc.

Halloween Pop-up Card

DESIGN BY **SUE ELDRED**

Card Exterior

Form a 5½ x 4¼-inch top-folded card from black card stock.

Card Front

1 Cut a 5 x 3¾-inch piece of Orange Swirls printed paper and a 5 x 2¼-inch piece of Purple Stripe printed paper; center and adhere purple paper to orange paper.

2 Cut a 5¼ x 4-inch piece of purple card stock; center and adhere printed-paper panel formed in step 1 to card stock. Center and adhere card stock to card front.

3 Referring to photo throughout, apply "Bubble, Bubble" and "Toil & Trouble" rub-on transfers to orange margins at top and bottom of card front.

4 Adhere "Trick or Treat" and Skeleton adhesive chipboard stickers to purple printed paper on card front as shown.

Card Interior

1 Adhere Mummy and Frankenstein stickers to black card stock; trim closely around each sticker.

2 Cut a 5¼ x 8¼-inch piece of Orange Swirls printed paper; fold in half, right sides facing, to form background of card interior.

3 Cut a 5¼ x 4⅛-inch piece of Green Dots printed paper; adhere to right side of Orange Swirls printed paper with bottom and side edges even. Fold card interior closed.

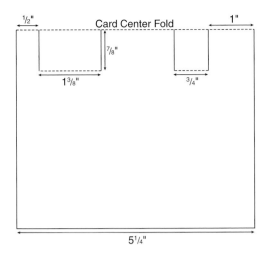

Halloween Pop-up

Materials

Card stock: black, purple
Printed paper: Halloween Orange Swirls,
  Halloween Green Dots, Halloween
  Purple Stripe
Halloween Adhesive Chipboard Words
Halloween Boy Grand Adhesion stickers
Halloween Border rub-on transfer
Craft knife and cutting mat
Double-sided tape

4 *Pop-up tabs:* With card interior closed, use craft knife to make cuts through fold and perpendicular to it, referring to diagram for placement. Open card interior and fold closed again, pushing pop-up tabs to inside.

5 Adhere double-sided tape to top half of card interior, avoiding pop-up tabs; insert into card and adhere. Adhere double-sided tape to bottom half of card interior; press onto card.

6 Adhere Mummy and Frankenstein stickers to front of pop-up tabs as shown, leaving a little space at bottom of stickers so card will close smoothly.

7 Cut 5¼ x 1¼-inch strip of Purple Stripe printed paper and a 5¼ x ¾-inch strip of Orange Swirls printed paper; center and adhere

paper to purple paper. Adhere paper strip inside card ⅝ inch from bottom. Stamp sentiment onto Orange Swirls strip.

8 Adhere "I Want Candy" sticker to card as shown; embellish background with bat and "Trick or Treat" rub-on transfers and dimensional candy stickers. ✸

Source: Printed papers, chipboard words, stickers and rub-on transfer from K&Company.

Words of Thanks

DESIGN BY **LAURA NICHOLAS,** COURTESY OF HOT OFF THE PRESS

Project Note

Adhere elements using Ultimate Glue unless instructed otherwise.

1 With fold at left, fold right edge of card front back toward fold so that all but ⅛ inch is overlapped.

2 Cut a 2½ x 6-inch piece of leaves printed paper; ink edges and adhere to card front under folded-back section.

3 Cut a 2⅜ x 6-inch piece of gold striped printed paper with stripes running horizontally; ink edges. Attach brown brads in corners and adhere paper to folded-back flap on card front.

4 Chalk veins of a large dark orange leaf; referring to photo throughout, center on card front and adhere to left flap only using glue dots.

5 Hand-print, or use computer to generate, "Words of Thanks!" or other sentiment onto tan card stock to fit within an area approximately 1 x 1½ inches. Trace tag shape around sentiment using template; cut out and ink edges. Adhere tag to left front flap as shown, tucking it under leaf.
Tie a bow from ribbon; adhere to leaf as shown using glue dots.

Card Interior

1 Trim ½ inch off right edge of card's back flap. Cut 2 x 6½-inch piece of leaves printed paper; ink edges and adhere inside card with right edges even.

2 Chalk veins of yellow and brown leaves. Adhere yellow leaf near bottom of leaves printed paper using glue dots.

3 *Pop-up block:* Cut a 3½ x 1-inch piece of black card stock. Score strip vertically ½ inch, 1¼ inches, 2 inches and 2¾ inches from left edge. Fold scored strip into an open-ended block, adhering overlapping ends. Referring to Fig. 1, adhere pop-up block inside card against fold about 2 inches from top so that block will collapse along scored lines, flattening completely, when card is closed.

4 Cut a 1¾ x 3-inch piece of leaves printed paper; ink edges. Adhere to tan card stock and cut out, leaving very narrow borders; ink edges again. Adhere leaves panel to pop-up block inside card.

5 Hand-print, or use computer to generate, "Gratitude," "Appreciation" and "Thankful!" on card stock. Cut rectangles around words; ink edges.

6 Adhere "Gratitude" to leaves panel on pop-up block; adhere small brown silk leaf.

7 Adhere remaining words inside card as shown using adhesive foam tape. ✳

Sources: Printed paper, brad pack, leaves, ribbon, tags template and glue from Hot Off The Press.

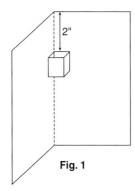

2"

Fig. 1

Materials

5 x 6½-inch white side-folded card
Tan card stock
Autumn Background printed papers
Brown ink pad
Brown chalk
Fine-tip black marker
Autumn Brad Pack
Cardmaker's Earth's Palette brown grosgrain ribbon
Silk leaves
Tags template
Artsy Collage Ultimate Glue
Small glue dots
Computer with font and printer (optional)

Santa Pop-up Card

DESIGN BY **SUE ELDRED**

Card Exterior
Form a 5½ x 4¼-inch top-folded card from dark turquoise card stock.

Card Front
1 Cut a 5 x 3¾-inch piece each of I Believe and Snowflake Patches printed papers. Tearing toward you, tear Snowflake Patches piece in half horizontally; adhere torn piece to I Believe printed paper with side and bottom edges even.

2 Cut a 5¼ x 4-inch piece of light green card stock; center and adhere printed paper panel formed in step 1 to card stock. Center and adhere card stock to card front.

3 Referring to photo throughout, adhere reindeer stickers to card front; stamp sentiment onto card front between reindeer.

Card Interior
1 Adhere Santa, Christmas Tree and Santa's Bag stickers to cream card stock; trim closely around each sticker.

2 Cut a 5¼ x 8¼-inch piece of Snowflake Patches printed paper; fold in half, right sides facing, to form background of card interior.

3 Cut a 5¼ x 4⅛-inch piece of I Believe printed paper; adhere to right side of Snowflake Patches printed paper with top and side edges even. Fold card interior closed.

4 *Pop-up tabs:* With card interior closed, use craft knife to make cuts through fold and perpendicular to it, referring to diagram for placement. Open card interior and fold closed again, pushing pop-up tabs to inside.

5 Adhere double-sided tape to top half of card interior, avoiding pop-up tabs; insert into card and adhere. Adhere double-sided tape to bottom half of card interior; press onto card.

6 Adhere stickers to front of pop-up tabs as shown, leaving a little space at bottom of stickers so card will close smoothly.

7 Stamp greeting onto cream card stock; trim around stamped image and adhere to dark turquoise card stock. Trim, leaving narrow borders. Adhere stamped sentiment to interior of card near upper left corner.

8 Cut 5¼ x ¾-inch strip of Poinsettia Flourish printed paper; adhere inside card ¾ inch from bottom. Stamp sentiment onto Poinsettia Flourish strip.

9 Embellish card with remaining stickers as desired, placing them carefully so that card will close evenly. ✳

Sources: Printed papers and stickers from K&Company; stamp sets from Hero Arts.

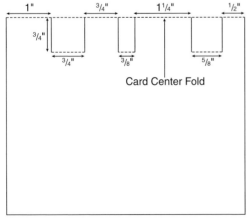

Santa Pop-up

Materials

Card stock: dark turquoise, light green, cream
Printed paper: I Believe, Snowflake Patches, Poinsettia Flourish
Peppermint Twist Santa Grand Adhesions
Stamp sets: Flourish Seasonal Messages, Joys of the Season
Black ink pad
Craft knife and cutting mat
Double-sided tape

Merry Christmas Pop-up Card

DESIGN BY **JERRY STEVENS**, COURTESY OF PLANE CLASS

The real Christmas spirit
with its warm and loving glow
comes from greeting friends like you—
The ones we're glad to know!

Project Note

Adhere elements using paper adhesive unless instructed otherwise.

1 Form a top-folded card at least 5½ x 4¼ inches from card stock. Open card; lay on cutting mat with inner surface facing up.

2 Center the template on the open card by aligning the notches on the ends of the template with the fold. Adhere template to card stock using removable tape.

3 Holding the craft knife perpendicular to card stock, cut all edges around letters. Note: When cutting slits that meet to form a corner, cut from the corner out in both directions to ensure a clean cut and sharp corner. As you cut card stock in waste areas free, stab it with the tip of your craft knife and lift it out. If it does not lift out effortlessly, carefully re-cut edges as needed.

4 When cutting long, narrow triangles such as those found when cutting the letters A, N, M and so on, always cut toward the sharpest point of the triangle first to reduce the chance of tearing.

5 As you become more accomplished, you will find it quicker to make all the cuts in a given direction, then rotate the cutting pad and card 90 degrees and make all the cuts in that direction; then rotate it 90 degrees again and make all cuts in that direction; and finally rotate it once more to make all remaining cuts. All waste pieces should come out easily.

6 When cutting is completed, remove template and tape. Carefully slide Folding Aid under cut letters and over outer edges of card. At the same time, position straight edge of template along bottom of cut letters.

7 While holding the template with one hand, push the Folding Aid up and over with the other hand, allowing the letters to crease. Apply pressure only to the Folding Aid, not the card; the Folding Aid will take the letters with it.

8 Reverse the card and repeat to bend the tops of the letters.

9 While holding the card, crease the tops and bottoms of the letters between your thumb and finger. Then place card on flat surface and complete the crease by rolling with the roller creaser.

10 Embellish card as desired with stickers. ✺

Source: Peel-off stickers, template, folding aid and creaser from POP-UPs by Plane Class.

Materials

Card stock
Starform metallic Christmas stickers
Merry Christmas POP-UP template
Folding Aid
Craft knife with #16 blade
Cutting mat
Roller creaser
Removable tape
Paper adhesive

Happy Birthday
Pop-up Card

DESIGN BY **JERRY STEVENS,** COURTESY OF PLANE CLASS

Project Note

Adhere elements using paper adhesive unless instructed otherwise.

1 Form a top-folded card at least 5½ x 4¼ inches from card stock. Open card; lay on cutting mat with inner surface facing up.

2 Center the template on the open card by aligning the notches on the ends of the template with the fold. Adhere template to card stock using removable tape.

3 Holding the craft knife perpendicular to card stock, cut all edges around letters. Note: When cutting slits that meet to form a corner, cut from the corner out in both directions to ensure a clean cut and sharp corner. As you cut card stock in waste areas free, stab it with the tip of your craft knife and lift it out. If it does not lift out effortlessly, carefully re-cut edges as needed.

4 When cutting long, narrow triangles such as those found when cutting the letters A, Y and so on, always cut toward the sharpest point of the triangle first to reduce the chance of tearing

5 As you become more accomplished, you will find it quicker to make all the cuts in a given direction, then rotate the cutting pad and card 90 degrees and make all the cuts in that direction; then rotate it 90 degrees again and make all cuts in that direction; and finally rotate it once more to make all remaining cuts. All waste pieces should come out easily.

6 When cutting is completed, remove template and tape. Carefully slide Folding Aid under cut letters and over outer edges of card. At the same time, position straight edge of template along bottom of cut letters.

7 While holding the template with one hand, push the Folding Aid up and over with the other hand, allowing the letters to crease. Apply pressure only to the Folding Aid, not the card; the Folding Aid will take the letters with it.

8 Reverse the card and repeat to bend the tops of the letters.

9 While holding the card crease the tops and bottoms of the letters between your thumb and finger. Then place card on flat surface and complete the crease by rolling with the roller creaser.

10 Embellish card as desired with stickers and printed paper motifs. Adhere butterfly sticker using adhesive foam squares for added dimension. ❋

Sources: Printed paper from K&Company; peel-off stickers, template, folding aid and creaser from POP-UPs by Plane Class.

Materials

Card stock
Printed paper
Starform metallic stickers: butterfly, birthday-themed
Happy Birthday POP-UP template
Folding Aid
Craft knife with #16 blade
Cutting mat
Roller creaser
Removable tape
Double-sided adhesive foam squares
Paper adhesive

Snowflake Accordion
CONTINUED FROM PAGE 107

Snowflake Embossing Pattern

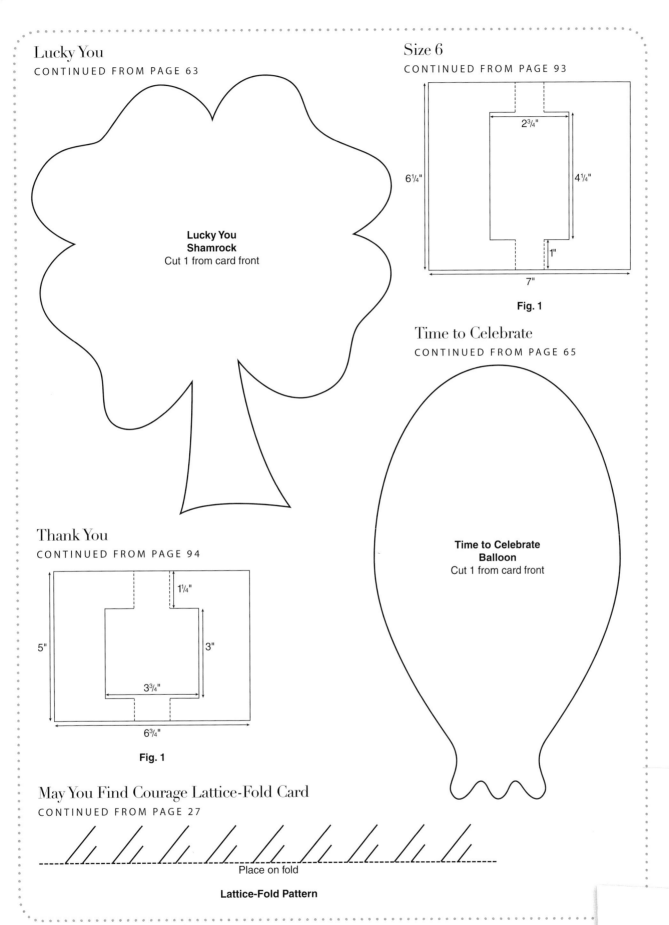

Lucky You
CONTINUED FROM PAGE 63

**Lucky You
Shamrock**
Cut 1 from card front

Size 6
CONTINUED FROM PAGE 93

2³/₄"

6¹/₄"

4¹/₄"

1"

7"

Fig. 1

Time to Celebrate
CONTINUED FROM PAGE 65

**Time to Celebrate
Balloon**
Cut 1 from card front

Thank You
CONTINUED FROM PAGE 94

1¹/₄"

5"

3"

3³/₄"

6³/₄"

Fig. 1

May You Find Courage Lattice-Fold Card
CONTINUED FROM PAGE 27

Place on fold

Lattice-Fold Pattern

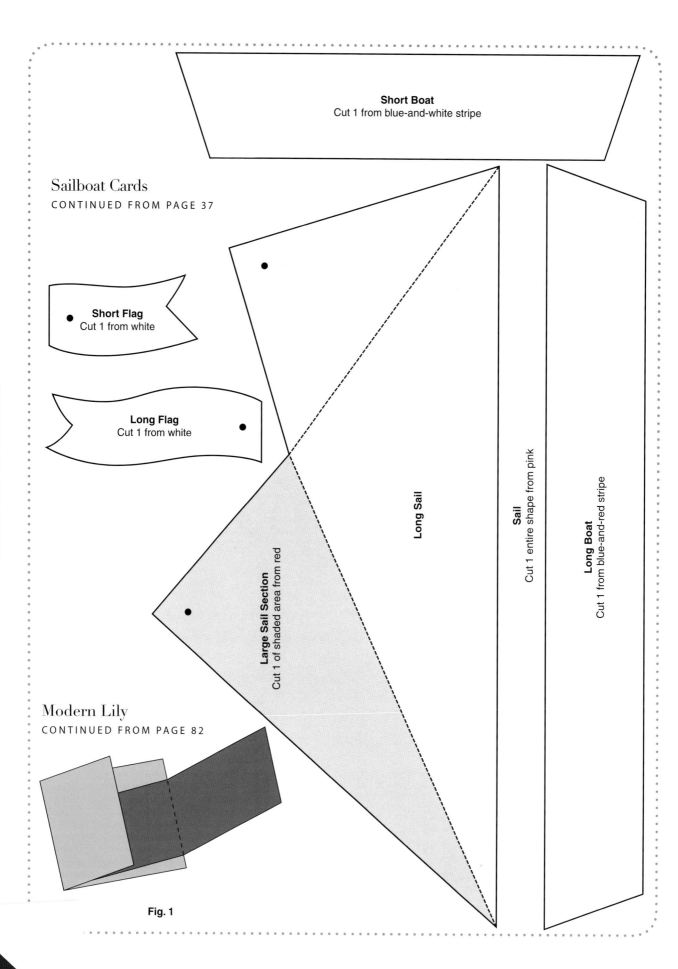

Short Boat
Cut 1 from blue-and-white stripe

Sailboat Cards
CONTINUED FROM PAGE 37

Short Flag
Cut 1 from white

Long Flag
Cut 1 from white

Long Sail

Sail
Cut 1 entire shape from pink

Long Boat
Cut 1 from blue-and-red stripe

Large Sail Section
Cut 1 of shaded area from red

Modern Lily
CONTINUED FROM PAGE 82

Fig. 1

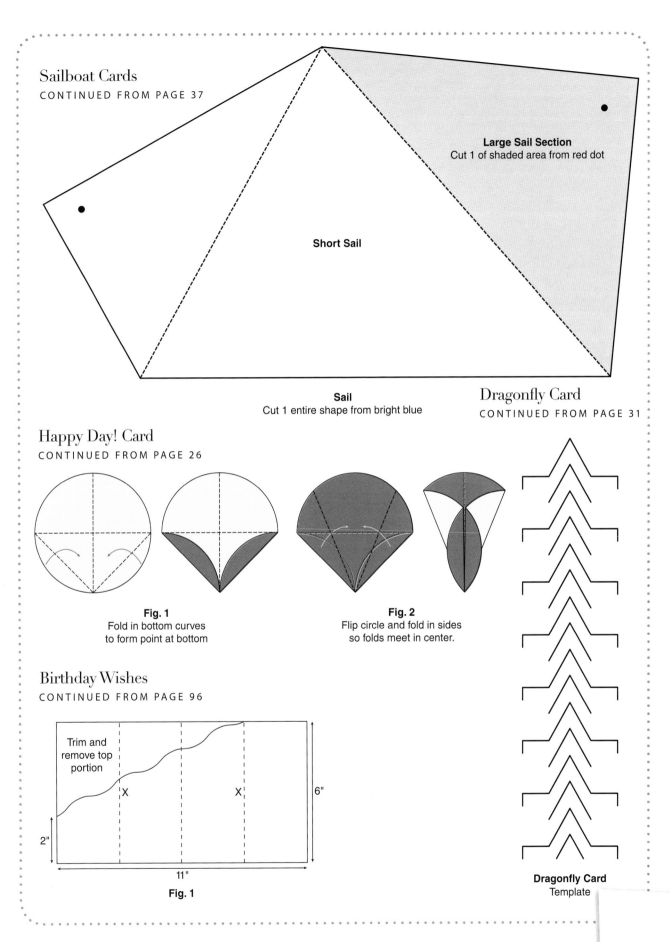

Sailboat Cards
CONTINUED FROM PAGE 37

Large Sail Section
Cut 1 of shaded area from red dot

Short Sail

Sail
Cut 1 entire shape from bright blue

Dragonfly Card
CONTINUED FROM PAGE 31

Happy Day! Card
CONTINUED FROM PAGE 26

Fig. 1
Fold in bottom curves
to form point at bottom

Fig. 2
Flip circle and fold in sides
so folds meet in center.

Birthday Wishes
CONTINUED FROM PAGE 96

Trim and
remove top
portion

X

X

6"

2"

11"

Fig. 1

Dragonfly Card
Template

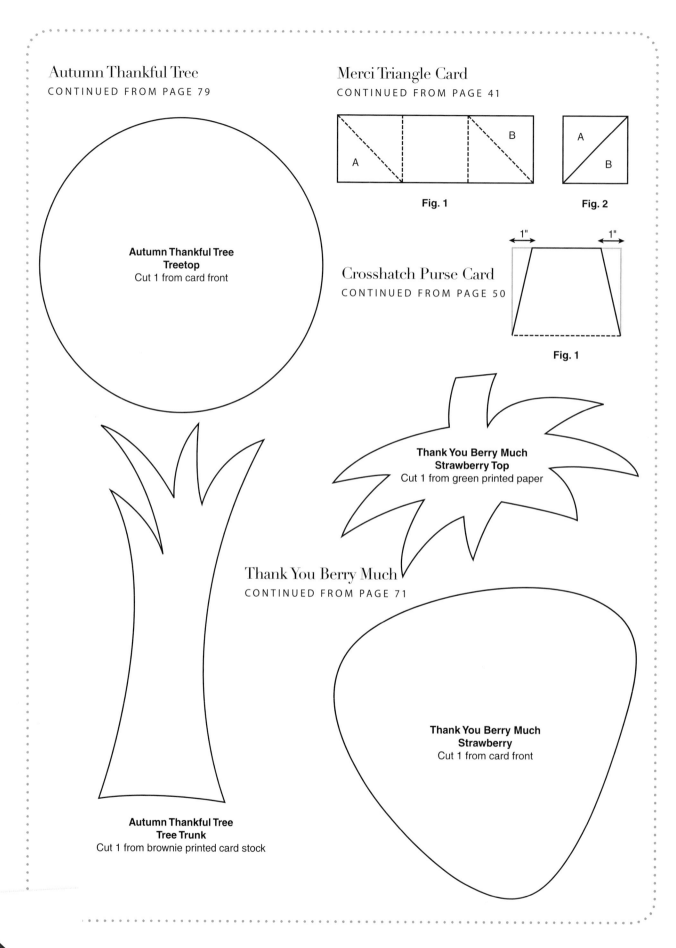

Autumn Thankful Tree
CONTINUED FROM PAGE 79

**Autumn Thankful Tree
Treetop**
Cut 1 from card front

Merci Triangle Card
CONTINUED FROM PAGE 41

A

B

Fig. 1

A

B

Fig. 2

1"   1"

Crosshatch Purse Card
CONTINUED FROM PAGE 50

Fig. 1

**Thank You Berry Much
Strawberry Top**
Cut 1 from green printed paper

Thank You Berry Much
CONTINUED FROM PAGE 71

**Thank You Berry Much
Strawberry**
Cut 1 from card front

**Autumn Thankful Tree
Tree Trunk**
Cut 1 from brownie printed card stock

BUYER'S GUIDE

Projects in this book were made using products provided by the manufacturers listed below. Look for the suggested products in your local craft- and art-supply stores. If unavailable, contact suppliers below. Some may be able to sell products directly to you; others may be able to refer you to retail sources.

3 Birds
www.3birdsdesign.com

7gypsies
(877) 7GYPSY7 (749-7797)
www.sevengypsies.com

A2Z Essentials
(419) 663-2869
www.geta2z.com

A Muse Artstamps
(877) 783-4882
www.amuseartstamps.com

Adornit/Carolee's Creations
(435) 563-1100
www.adornit.com

American Crafts Inc.
(801) 226-0747
www.americancrafts.com

Anna Griffin Inc.
(888) 817-8170
www.annagriffin.com

Art Declassified
(248) 320-9487
www.artdeclassified.com

Art Institute Glitter
(877) 909-0805
www.artglitter.com

Artistic Outpost
www.artisticoutpost.com

Autumn Leaves
(800) 727-2727
www.autumnleaves.com

BasicGrey
(801) 544-1116
www.basicgrey.com

Bazzill Basics Paper
(800) 560-1610
www.bazzillbasics.com

Beacon Adhesives Inc.
(914) 699-3405
www.beaconcreates.com

Blumenthal Lansing Company
(563) 538-4211
www.buttonsplus.com

Boxer Scrapbook Productions
(888) 625-6255
www.boxerscrapbooks.com

Cards and Crafts
www.cardsandcrafts.freeservers.com

Chatterbox
(877) 749-7797
www.chatterboxinc.com

Clearsnap Inc.
(888) 448-4862
www.clearsnap.com

Close To My Heart
www.closetomyheart.com

Cloud 9 Design
(866) 348-5661
www.cloud9design.biz

ColorBox
(888) 448-4862
www.colorbox.com

Copic
(541) 684-0013
www.copicmarker.com

Coredinations
(866) 628-3715
www.coredinations.com

Cornish Heritage Farms
(877) 860-5328
www.cornishheritagefarms.com

Cosmo Cricket
(800) 852-8810
www.cosmocricket.com

Crafts Etc.
(800) 888-0321 ext. 1275
www.craftsetc.com

Craf-T Products
www.craf-tproducts.com

Crate Paper Inc.
(801) 798-8996
www.cratepaper.com

Creative Café
www.creativeimaginations.us

Creative Imaginations
(800) 942-6487
www.cigift.com

Creative Impressions
(719) 596-4860
www.creativeimpressions.com

Creative Memories
(800) 468-9335
www.creativememories.com

CutCardStock.com
(219) 787-8129
www.CutCardStock.com

Daisy D's Paper Co.
(888) 285-7575
www.daisyds.com

Déjà Views
(860) 243-0303
www.dejaviews.com

Destination Scrapbook Designs
(866) 806-7826
www.destinationstickers.com

Die Cuts With A View
(801) 224-6766
www.diecutswithaview.com

Doodlebug Design Inc.
www.doodlebug.ws

Dream Street Papers
(480) 275-9736
www.dreamstreetpapers.com

DYMO Corp.
global.dymo.com

Ecstasy Crafts Inc.
(888) 288-7131
www.ecstasycrafts.com

EK Success LTD.
www.eksuccess.com

Fiskars
(866) 348-5661
www.fiskarscrafts.com

Flair Designs
(360) 391-0898
www.flairdesigns.com

Forster Craft
www.homecrafting.com

Gina K Designs
(608) 579-1026
www.ginakdesigns.com

Graphic 45
(866) 573-4806
www.g45papers.com

Hampton Art
(800) 981-5169
www.hamptonart.com

Heidi Grace Designs
(866) 347-5277
www.heidigrace.com

Heidi Swapp/Advantus Corp.
(904) 482-0092
www.heidiswapp.com

Hero Arts
www.heroarts.com

Hot Off The Press
(888) 300-3406
www.paperwishes.com

Imaginisce
(801) 908-8111
www.imaginisce.com

Inkadinkado
(800) 523-8452
www.inkadinkado.com

Inque Botique Inc./Darice Inc.
(866) 432-7423
www.darice.com

The Japanese Paper Place
(416) 538-9669
japanesepaperplace.com

Jenni Bowlin Studio
www.jennibowlin.com

K&Company
(888) 244-2083
www.kandcompany.com

Kaisercraft
www.kaisercraft.net

Karen Foster Design
(801) 326-1373
www.scrapbookpaper.com

KI Memories
(972) 243-5595
www.kimemories.com

Kokuyo
(800) 710-5526
www.expressivetraditions.com

Lasting Impressions for Paper Inc.
(800) 9-EMBOSS
www.lastingimpressions.com

Li'l Davis Designs
www.lildavisdesigns.com

Lizzie Anne Designs
(425) 844-3804
www.lizzieannedesigns.com

Luxe Designs
(972) 573-2120
www.luxedesigns.com

Magenta Rubber Stamps
(450) 922-5253
www.magentarubberstamps.com

Magic Mesh
(651) 345-6374
www.magicmesh.com

Making Memories
(801) 294-0430
www.makingmemories.com

Marco's Paper
(888) 433-5239
www.marcopaper.com

Mark Richards Inc.
(888) 901-0091
www.markrichardsusa.com

Martha Stewart: Crafts
(877) 882-0319
www.marthastewartcrafts.com

May Arts
www.mayarts.com

Maya Road
(877) 427-7764
www.mayaroad.com

McGill Inc.
(800) 982-9884
www.mcgillinc.com

me & my BIG ideas
(949) 583-2065
www.meandmybigideas.com

Melissa Frances/Heart & Home Collectables Inc.
(905) 686-3031
(888) 616-6166
www.melissafrances.com
www.heartandhome.com

Memory Box
www.memorywboxco.com

Michaels
(800) MICHAELS (642-4235)
www.michaels.com

Mrs. Grossman's
(800) 429-4549
www.mrsgrossmans.com

My Mind's Eye
(800) 665-5116
www.mymindseye.com

Neenah
(888) 631-9170
www.paperworks.com

October Afternoon
(866) 513-5553
www.octoberafternoon.com

Offray & Son Inc.
www.offray.com

Paper Adventures
(973) 406-5000
www.anwcrestwood.com/pa

The Paper Company
(973) 406-5000
www.anwcrestwood.com/tpc

Paper Inspirations
www.paperinspirations.com

Paper Parachute
(503) 533-4513
www.paperparachute.com

Paper Pizzazz

Paper Salon Inc.
(800) 627-2648
www.papersalon.com

Paper Studio
(480) 557-5700
www.paperstudio.com

Papertrey Ink
www.papertreyink.com

Pebbles Inc.
(800) 438-8153
www.pebblesinc.com

Piggy Tales
(702) 755-8600
www.piggytales.com

Pink Paislee
(816) 729-6124
www.pinkpaislee.com

Plaid Enterprises Inc./All Night Media
(800) 842-4197
www.plaidonline.com

POP-Ups by Plane Class
(888) 750-5276
www.popuptemplates.com

Prima Marketing Inc.
(909) 627-5532
www.primamarketinginc.com

Prism Papers
(866) 902-1002
www.prismpapers.com

Provo Craft/Coluzzle
mail-order source:
Creative Express
(800) 937-7686
www.provocraft.com

The Punch Bunch
(254) 791-4209
www.thepunchbunch.com

Queen & Co.
www.queenandco.com

Quietfire Design
www.quietfiredesign.com

Ranger Industries Inc.
(732) 389-3535
www.rangerink.com

Rubbernecker
(909) 263-9322
www.rubbernecker.com

Rubber Stampede/Delta
(800) 423-4135
www.deltacreative.com

Rusty Pickle
(801) 746-1045
www.rustypickle.com

Sakura Hobby Craft
(310) 212-7878
www.sakuracraft.com

Sassafras Lass
(801) 269-1331
www.sassafraslass.com

Scenic Route Paper Co.
(801) 542-8071
www.scenicroutepaper.com

Scor-Pal Products
(877) 629-9908
www.scor-pal.com

Scrapworks Inc.
(801) 363-1010
www.scrapworks.com

Scrappy Cat
(440) 234-4850
www.scrappycatonline.com

Search Press
www.searchpress.com

SEI
(800) 333-3279
www.shopsei.com

Sharpie
(800) 323-0749
www.sharpie.com

Sizzix/Ellison
(877) 355-4766
www.sizzix.com

Spellbinders Paper Arts.
(888) 547-0400
www.spellbinders.us

Spica

Stamp N Plus Scrap N
(715) 271-1873
www.powderedchalk.com

Stampendous Inc.
(800) 869-0474
www.stampendous.com

Stampin' Up!
(800) STAMP-UP (782-6787)
www.stampinup.com

Stamps by Judith
www.stampsbyjudith.com

Stemma/Masterpiece Studios
www.masterpiecestudios.com

Sweetwater
(970) 867-4428
www.sweetwaterscrapbook.com

Tonic Studios
(608) 836-4478
www.kushgrip.com

Tulip/Duncan Enterprises
(800) 438-6226
www.duncancrafts.com

Tsukineko Inc.
(425) 883-7733
www.tsukineko.com

Uchida of America
(800) 541-5877
www.marvy.com

Vap Scrap Stamps
www.craftywotname.com

Verve Visual
www.vervevisual.com

Webster's Pages
(800) 543-6104
www.websterspages.com

We R Memory Keepers
(801) PICK-WER (742-5937)
www.wermemorykeepers.com

Wild Asparagus

WorldWin Papers
(888) 843-6455
www.worldwinpapers.com

DESIGNER'S INDEX

The Scoop, p.113

Girlfriends, p.152